£10·99

UPCOMING CHANGES

CHANGES

THE NEXT 20 YEARS

UPCOMING CHANGES

CHANGES

THE NEXT 20 YEARS

A MICHAEL BOOK
BY

Joya Pope

EMERALD

WAVE

Fayetteville, AR

Printed and bound in the United States of America.
Cover design and title pages by Karen Smelser.

First Printing, May 1992
Second Printing, updated, January 1993
ISBN 0-942531-33-7
$12.95

Emerald Wave Publishing Company
Box 969, Fayetteville, AR 72702

Dedication

To all the healers, seen and unseen—
most especially Duane.

Contents

Acknowledgments:

There are many people to thank for their support with this project. Janice Kegler helped me clarify what this, my second Michael book, was to be. Lia Marie Danks prompted me to begin the book, beautifully and smoothly as is her way (this about two minutes after I'd moved to Arkansas!). Lucille Crow spurred me on mid-stream and told me to hurry that it was important information to get out. My many conversations with Dan Vega, who has a profound sense of oneness with the Earth, its creatures and its changes, helped me stay clear-eyed and strong of heart while immersed in certain parts of this book. Ultimately because of him, I asked Michael better questions about environmental change and gained some inner understanding and peace sooner than I might have otherwise. His local television show, *One Whirled View,* aims his own brand of humor at environmental and political issues.

Big thanks must go to both Addie Adamson and Richard Villanueva for excellent, time-consuming editing and proofreading and to Virginia Manchester and Candace Marie for transcribing tapes which were never easy to transcribe. I very much appreciated Karen Smelser's patience and talent in bringing the cover to graphic life.

Duane Hall found himself without his pal and social partner as I disappeared into my Mac, but he gently kept me in good shape and good spirits nevertheless—though he too wished I could have hurried.

Thanks also go to Michael for unwavering support throughout this project and for being an incredible source.

Foreword

After experiencing and experimenting with many of the spiritual disciplines and growth offerings that became available in the 60s and 70s, I learned to channel. For the first ten years, I channeled my higher-self and some other wonderful beings who tended towards statements like, "Trust. Don't worry, we are with you." While this always felt extremely soothing on an energetic level, which I liked, I did not usually quit worrying about whatever it was I was worrying about. While I was receiving loving support, I obviously wasn't getting information or understanding which could help me grapple with the actual circumstances of life.

In 1984, with a strong desire for clear, specific, intellectually valid information, I asked for and began receiving communication from Michael. The depth and quality of my channeling radically changed. By 1987 I was completing my first book on Michael's material and my work had become writing, teaching and channeling, exclusively.

I have been arm deep in my Mac for the last year working on this book, convinced of the need for a realistic look at some of the prospects for the the next two decades. Both in the writing and in the private readings I do, my personal pleasure seems to come from being able to present a perspective which helps people breathe easier because life, warts and all, suddenly makes better sense—intellectually and emotionally. I hope the observations and ideas presented here will serve as useful steering for you and that it will help to keep our world stable and us inspired.

I was being internally pushed to write, or believe me, I'd have been out adventuring in my new part of the country much more often. And in fact I did receive, quite to my surprise, some strong prodding from Michael every so often when my proportion of fooling around was high compared to the time I was spending on this book.

We are ready to turn here, on a dime, and while not exactly towards world disaster, life could perhaps feel that way at times. You can position yourself for the 90s consciously or unconsciously. Conscious is usually better. How we all choose to view change and manage it, whether growing and transform-ing, or withdrawing and shutting down, becomes the passage-way not only to our individual futures, but to our collective future as well, and another major reason for this book.

Joya Pope

A note on English usage:

Most Michael channeling became direct, that is, oral, years ago. At that point the English started sounding more natural than the Ouija-board formality of the earliest Michael books, the *Messages from Michael* series by Chelsea Quinn Yarbro.

Spoken communication, channeling included, doesn't often make for an ideal page. Speaking and writing are very different forms of communication. What you have in your hands is the result of my work with the reams of material channeled for this book. It remains true to the channeling in tone, vein, spirit and detail. Except for the footnotes, which are my explanatory additions, it is written in Michael's voice.

I had best make a few points here about pronoun usage. Michael, as you may know, is not an individual, but the group consciousness of just over a thousand souls who have completed all earth lifetimes and are now teaching from another plane of existence, two steps away from this, the physical plane. In conversation, I refer to the group energy that is "Michael" as "he" (and not "they"), because that is what makes sense in English. Michael, however, refers to himself as "we", which is how the text reads because it is in his voice.

Instead of using only male pronouns to refer to humans of both sexes, or the cumbersome he/she, him/her, etc., one or the other, male or female, is used here interchangeably.

And when old words die out on the tongue,
new melodies break forth from the heart;
and where the old tracks are lost, new country
is revealed with its wonders.
—Rabindranath Tagore, *Gitanjali*

CHAPTER 1

Old Pattern, New Pattern?
Some Pattern, No Pattern?

Revolutions are not made: they come. A revolution is
as natural a growth as an oak. It comes out of the past.
Its foundations are laid far back.
—*Wendell Phillips*

May you live in interesting times.
—*Chinese curse*

NEW VISION

This is a great time and a dangerous time. The world's
ways are changing, rapidly; the old story is being rewritten,
along with the tune. Thank your higher selves for having you
alive and roaming around during these milepost decades of
human evolutionary history (though at nearly six billion, the
whole gang is pretty much collected). You all desired to sample

and savor the sweeping changes of this highly consequential era, but it is likely you are also here to work to change the world, to accelerate, or perhaps ease, these late-century developments, and to protect your future as you create it.

Tales of great social and political change are in your newspapers and your faces daily. The Berlin wall is out-of-order, apartheid breaking apart, the Soviet Union broken. Eastern Europe won enough freedom to hang itself or fly, and is busily doing both. More and more people are refusing to be denied their basic rights: The Russian people courageously felled a coup by the old boys; Anita Hill gave American women the focus to fell even more good old boys and ways; incest popped out of the back room and on to the discussion table; Los Angeles erupted after the judicial system once again ignored racially-oriented police violence. The United Nations suddenly has vitality and some clout; Amnesty International is no longer half-gagged, but enjoying new potency.

Western Europe is plugging away on millions of differences, aiming to unite under one economic banner to grow stronger and richer. There is little toleration suddenly for financial corruption in high places; worldwide, politicians fumble in bright view, making ethics a newly interesting subject. Even the unprincipled, monetarily entrenched healthcare system in the U.S. is getting the critical attention it deserves. Environmental problems abound and ecological disasters pend, still just out of sight despite the world's first Earth Summit.

Any period of great metamorphosis tends to cause formidable economic problems, for financial systems march easily with stability, not with change. The long-rich United States is already stumbling, its economy unglued, but then Western Europe and Japan are having their money issues too. The impetuous spending of the 80s now seems excessive, even downright dangerous, to millions of former spending addicts.

So what about Peace and a Golden New Age you say?

Well, you will savor hints of both, but for now the transition phase itself will continue grabbing your attention in a fairly satisfying way. Reality is going to look pretty fascinating—and remain pretty fluid. Certainly you have a challenging interval here, but still it is a period bound to thrill most of our readers to their very cores because of the major value changes which deliver needed relief to all life on the planet. The 90s will bring to an abrupt end many old ways of thinking and see the emergence of many new approaches to collective life on earth. Already you are living in a quickly shifting borderland between one age and another. The five mid-decade years will see much disintegration and breakdown, but will also be years when high feelings, creativity and social innovation open many new doors.

It is specifically this new vision and novel trailblazing that will keep these mid-decade years from feeling like the Great Depression, an era when people went into a gray survival mode. The sense now is: We are letting go of a lot, but a lot was rotten and needed to go; out of this pain and hardship we are building a new, more workable society and giving the earth a chance to heal. People will be asking very basic questions like: How do you get all children nourished and educated, and adults productive and happy? What kinds of systems support people, motivate them and bring out their best? What is affordable? What saves the Earth? And even: How can I help; what is my part in this?

CHICKEN OR THE EGG?

Mass consciousness is in the process of changing significantly. Major inner changes are always reflected in the physical world. The first and primary shift we see is a shift in consciousness; from that all else follows. And, humanity right now is experiencing one of the most momentous and interesting transitions in consciousness (the way it thinks and feels and acts) that it will ever make.

For the most part, the future can best be spoken of in terms of probabilities, simply because people create it and people have a certain degree of free will to change it while they are on the planet. Collectively humans create policies, modify events, and the future. From our perspective at this point in time, it appears highly improbable that this decade, or any of the next few, will be as apocalyptic as Nostradamus, Edgar Cayce, or many others have predicted. Humanity has obviously moved along a little better than earlier expected.

Nevertheless, the planet is due for an increasing degree of foundation rattling, provoked by volcanic and earthquake activity, harsher weather patterns, subsequent economic downturns, food shortages, insect surges and new health concerns. While this may appear more Gray 90s than Gay, in retrospect the decade will stir fondness because people will have discovered more fulfilling ways of living, personally and also within their local and world communities.

We want to speak to you in fair detail about the nature of this consciousness change itself, as well as about how it will manifest in the world. We'll discuss the ways in which the Earth itself is pushing these changes along. And we wish to speak to you about developing a perspective and a personal spirituality that is neither magical thinking—burying a saint's statue head down in the yard until your favor is granted—nor a blind faith that exiles your intellect, and responsibility, to the back forty—the Space Brothers are coming to save "us" from this mess. Peace means being centered, serene during the storm, not taking yourself, guns, dogs and dehydrated foods to some survivalist's haven only to be perpetually on guard.

Many of the coming years will be exciting; all will be challenging. The more centered you can remain, the more creative you will be and the more happy to be alive—and then, you will be doing your part to bring about a peaceful shift.

CHAPTER 2

Mass Consciousness
The Shift of the 90s

The 1990s sure aren't like the 1980s.
—Donald Trump

The decade is not about economic hardship or geological
stirrings, though both will be troublesome, but about
resourcefulness, about new ways of realizing common
human goals. The 90s are about evolution, but an evolution
provoked by inspiration every bit as much as by adversity.
—Michael

A WORD ABOUT CONSCIOUSNESS

Consciousness is everything; it all starts there. If you feel stuck, helpless and sure that nothing you do will ever make a difference, then you aren't likely to change your diet for the better, learn to meditate, prepare for new work—or even prop up the sagging porch or plug the cracks in the wall the wind sings through. On the other hand, if you feel what you do does make a difference, you are immediately empowered, more lively and upbeat and, no surprise, the quality of your life does improve.

While what we see changing in mass consciousness doesn't fit neatly into this helpless/empowered dichotomy, the example does demonstrate how consciousness works and why it's important. Consciousness comes from inside you, from your soul or essence, as well the past life experience and wisdom you carry with you. It comes also from the personality traits you chose to work with this lifetime: Some people are born upbeat, others cynical; some may look at life with such caution that they hardly move, while others are aggressive and quick. Your consciousness is also affected by the mind-set of others, most especially your parents, and by your society's values.

Some lifetimes are slow, full of little but dull repetition; others flow comfortably; still others move with ground-shaking quickness, continually packing in major experience and growth. Sometimes a person, or society, is able to breeze along, easily stretching to adjust as circumstances change. Other times, change drags a person or country with it, kicking, complaining, and getting pretty grouchy. The human personality is almost always happier with a little foreshadowing, which allows it to anticipate and prepare.

CHANGING GEARS AFTER 2500 YEARS

The 90s will birth about as much change in the way people think and act and as much consciousness growth as the last four decades put together. Given the last four decades, this is bound to be difficult to conceive. The pace of the 20th century is still increasing, pushing people and their social systems to grow quickly and then be ready to move on again. Political systems will be panting to catch up. The first decade of the 21st century will see plenty of action and growth too, but many of the changes of those years will be consciously created out of the slam-bam education endured in the 90s.

Consciousness, whether individual or collective, tends to have a life of its own. For instance, the hyper-materialism of the 80s will likely cause those years to remain known as the "Greed Decade". Crave, buy, charge and steal material goods, show them off and enjoy them; these were the values that permeated the air. Apparently the U.S. and a good part of the Western world needed one last gagging look at me-first materialism before something new could truly emerge.

The 90s are not about greed; probably you realize that already. Awareness is growing that present systems—political, environmental, educational, economic and social—are out-of-date, not handling increasing levels of problems. Many are already breaking down of their own accord or by their own corruption. The times are ripe for a primary rearrangement of human priorities. Getting rid of so much that is old may mean "Detox Decade" will be the label that eventually sticks on the 90s. Already that label makes sense for what most of Eastern Europe and the former U.S.S.R. are going through.

The five mid-decade years especially will see incredibly fast movement, a monumental shift really, in the way humans live, act and interact. Shifts of this magnitude don't happen often or at random on a planet; there is a predictable pattern, a sequence to epochal change of this nature (though having a sequence does not necessarily prevent chaos in-process).

Planet Earth is whipping headlong into her third major consciousness shift. This third shift is always the most intriguing and difficult juncture of all—on any planet.[1] In order to throw some light on current changes, it would be helpful first to briefly focus on each of the prior shifts in global consciousness.

CONSCIOUSNESS SHIFT #1
Earth's first major transition occurred back in what is pre-

---

[1] Every planet with sentient, conscious beings on it goes (grows) through the same patterns—even though the creatures are very different from humans, (peaceful, non-tool-users for instance).

history to you now when large numbers of your forebears began moving out of simple survival situations and consciousness and primitive agricultural or nomadic lives. Enough among them had mastered the natural world that they began collecting together, sharing the ideas that ultimately allowed more complex and interesting societies to develop. They saw that human existence could be made more dependable if people cooperated and became more orderly in their manner of living.

Consciousness is always reflected in life. As people moved towards cooperation and orderliness—first and foremost a consciousness shift—they gave birth to great agrarian civilizations of the Neolithic period. This movement away from loose bands and clans to more complicated communities was the first widespread social rearrangement in human cultural evolution. It provoked monumental changes in the way most people lived.

These early societies developed with the belief that if existence were carefully organized and everyone followed well-defined rules, life could be good for all. You controlled yourself, others if necessary, the environment to the degree possible, with the hope and belief that life would then flow smoothly. And in fact, people did begin to enjoy the security that a more regimented existence could give. Codes of laws were issued, dictionaries and encyclopedias compiled, calendars grew accurate, sundials came into being and many, many holidays and feast days were celebrated.

For the most part, the previous job description for all men was along the lines of hunting, protection and construction, while women gathered seasonal foods, invented agriculture, managed cooking and child-care and crafted baskets, pots, and clothing as needed. Now, with life becoming more organized, labor became more specialized. Societies developed to the point that people were able to become apprentices—and masters—in certain arenas, perhaps as a priestess, healer or midwife, or as an irrigation or agricultural specialist, animal expert, builder, or as a clay, metal or leather worker.

A predominantly goddess-oriented spirituality arose: God was a woman in all the places where these breakthroughs in social and material technology were made. The feminine principle tends naturally towards identity with life and nature, and, in fact, both were revered. The power of the Goddess was to give goodness to life, not to punish or exact obedience. Quite different from the Gods of the next consciousness period!

Because mere survival was no longer the issue, people became increasingly community centered. Lives became more assured and, as you can see from the art of the period, more celebratory. Times were so comfortable and truly civilized that most people were able to live without fortress walls surrounding their communities. In fact, throughout Europe, India, Mesopotamia and Arabia, village sites were most often chosen for beauty, good water, soil and pasture, not for their defensive value. The people of this era enjoyed the abundance they had brought to life, creating things of beauty and technologies of production, not destruction. When metals started being worked, they became decorative objects, religious items or tools, but not usually swords or spears.

As can still be seen from extant grave and housing sites, people shared without much hierarchy; women were perhaps a little more "on top", though in most places they didn't subjugate others, including men; nor did a class of priests, rulers, police or army exist to corner the wealth of these citizens. For thousands of years, many human societies were able to live with little social inequality or violence, in a manner quite different from the norm of the last several thousand years. These societies were so radically different from what followed that it became difficult for later generations to believe what they heard about life in the golden times.

"All good things were theirs. In peaceful ease they kept their lands with good abundance, rich in flocks and dear to the immortals." This is Hesiod, a Greek poet, describing what many of his time had heard rumored of a "golden race". Hesiod was in fact referring to these societies, which were by his time of 800 B.C. under severe stress, or just plain gone, scattered and demolished. Gods and spears were taking over from the Goddess.

It was difficult for the anthropologists of the 19th and 20th centuries to look at the physical evidence they'd dug up with unjaded eyes or free minds. To them, these unfortified societies looked weak and defenseless. They couldn't imagine that the lack of hierarchy might be a blessing; it was seen as primitive. The seeming importance given to women was too incomprehensible a notion to draw much of their attention. It is unusually difficult to think outside your cultural norms. Few manage.

"Let's cooperate, pay attention to rules and make our communities work for everybody." This was the type of consciousness that held sway on the earth from about 10,000 B.C. This lengthy and uneven transition period contained especial violence during the 1500 years before Christ.

These consciousness periods we are describing to you are not monolithic, with every community at all times exhibiting all these qualities, for always some societies and some individuals will be off doing their own things on different time schedules. Some areas will remain simpler, connecting with the values of the past, while some societies will move ahead, checking out what is next. Egypt, for example, shifted much earlier to a male-dominated, hierarchical form of organization which included slavery.[2] But still, the overall regard for rules, laws and cooperation were the new, compelling consciousness elements that pervaded these several thousand years and made quite a turnabout from the survival consciousness that most of the world had struggled with previously.

---

2 Atlantis was a highly structured, highly technological society that existed as an enclave in a fairly primitive world. It caused its own demise about 14,000 years ago.

CONSCIOUSNESS SHIFT #2

What changed? What caused the violence that pushed these societies out of existence? Consciousness, of course, and then people's actions. Change came from inside some societies, such as Egypt. In others it came from the outside. Remember those invading hordes of barbarians riding down from the North who wouldn't go away? Their Gods had swords. No reverence for mystical and religious experience here, not even much reverence for life; they terrified these pastoral communities, and destroyed them.

It was power they worshiped. They used their knowledge of metallurgy to make daggers, spears and swords. Warlike, destructive, and growing in numbers and ferocity, they invaded in waves, knocking out the countless settled communities of Old Europe and the Middle East, creating masses of refugees for well over one thousand years.

But it wasn't just barbarians from the North exhibiting newer, aggressive behaviors. People everywhere were starting to change. To many, the previous regard for structure and controlled behavior started to seem spiritless, impotent. That ambitious urge to dominate anything perceived to be weaker took hold early within some people, cultures and countries and later in others.

Phoenicians funneled their new sense of independence into exploration, colonies and trade; Assyria into the wars which ultimately ruined it. A great empire was formed in India. Some time after the Jews were roughly expelled from Egypt, they took Jerusalem for themselves, causing horrendous carnage along the way. Sparta made a life philosophy out of its warrior-like ways, and even pridefully experimented with chemical warfare. The Persians and Greeks fought everybody. Rome managed to do in the more peaceful Etruscans, and Alexander the Great began his conquest of the known world.

As chronic warfare, invasions and dislocations became par

for this period, the old partnership ways of thinking went. People started thinking individualistically and egotistically, not of the whole. This was the era of fortress and wall building, now necessary to keep out your enemies. The old attunement with nature disappeared, replaced by strong and dominating behaviors which often worked to the detriment of the natural world. The new consciousness counseled, Search out your own advantage in every situation; the weak deserve contempt. Winner take all and power to him. (Typically, people in women's bodies weren't so easily able to take direct advantage of this shift in values.)[3]

As unpleasant as this all might seem, it was not a wrong turn for history but a normal part of a larger growth experience that had many positive points as well as the obvious negatives. This third period always sees a move away from rules, structure and sense of community into more pushy, aggressive, individualistic ways of being. Individuals do grow through these behaviors, becoming more assured, energetic beings. They aren't as kind to each other, though, since impressing their will on the world suddenly takes precedence over most other kinds of actions.

On any planet with sentient life, the self-aware creatures must first work through survival issues on their planet; and then work on creating order and predictability. Once this civilizing phase is handled, it is time to move on, to push every limit and see what can be gained. On the positive side, it is a move into a fearless kind of thinking which encourages individuation, daring exploration, intellectual innovation, and often even includes the drive and discipline to get what you want.

As you can see, the earth is currently reeling from exactly these narrowly focused, egocentric behaviors. On a planet as actively aggressive as Earth, this consciousness stage is bound to be

---

3 Riane Eisler's book, *The Chalice & The Blade,* beautifully describes both the Neolithic period and goddess worship as well as the crushing of those agrarian communities. Michael says she has somewhat over-idealized the era, but that it is an excellent antidote to what male historians and anthropologists have traditionally done.

bloody, and ultimately thrust the very survival of the planet into question through warfare and unthinking assaults on resources.

CONSCIOUSNESS SHIFT #3

The transition of the 90s will move people amazingly far from the individualistic thinking that says the strongest person or country gets to dominate towards a world where partnership, compassion and conscience will once again flourish. As will communication, creativity, kindness, intimacy, arguments, emotional aches, pains, and considerations of all kinds—but more on that later.

Being on top, having it all, ultimately leaves a bewildering, lonely spot, which starts calling ever more attention to itself. That's Earth now, with this voice getting louder and louder; materialism doesn't feel so satisfying. Looking only to one's own or one's country's advantage doesn't have the same cachet as before. People will be busily redefining who is part of their "big family" and who is not, with the thrust of consciousness being towards making the "family" as inclusive as possible.

An extraordinary factor in the present shift is its speed, because this new perceptivity is coming on strong, strong enough to penetrate many societies all around the world during the decade. This newer consciousness has been filtering in, affecting many people since the 20s. In the 60s, it became more noticeable and compelling. After 1987 (yes, Harmonic Convergence time) it was set in place. What the 90s are bringing is a short, intense transition into the new era. This is a turnabout time, a time of many far-reaching changes.

Some change will come as a crash course, chaotic and harsh, as it did to Eastern Europe. The disassembling U.S.S.R. has had its excitement and elation also, but is faced with many problems—problems which could be fanned into ethnic hatred and miserable wars or settled with communication, compromise and a perspective which keeps the whole in mind. With these countries, you have been seeing changes being made at the breakneck speeds which will be typical of the 90s. People everywhere will become impassioned, pushing their societies towards fairer forms of governance, equitable solutions to money, health care, education and towards more environmental integrity.

Change means life isn't stable, and we are talking about monumental changes continuing to roll throughout this decade. A person's mind can understand change and theoretically adjust, perhaps even being glad for it, but the body itself and the personality are bound to regret loss of the old stability and predictability. Our interest in putting out an overview of the coming decades is that it will tend to anchor people, and help make the seeming turnabouts less distressing. We aim to take away some of the shock, and by pointing towards the bigger picture (basically the vast improvement in the way life will be lived and shared) we expect to be able to help minds and spirits stay positive. And, we want to remind you all that awareness and flexibility are especially useful in a fast current.

NEW CONSCIOUSNESS

With this new consciousness coming onto center stage, you will see greater environmental respect, politics turning more liberal and practical, business ethics coming under increasingly strong scrutiny, education becoming more creative and interesting, animal rights an increasingly hot issue and a continued examination of relationships in all their permutations, glorious and inglorious. The third world is likely to receive closer attention, with more aid getting to the people who need it in a way which provokes beneficial social change.

If this consciousness shift had even a hundred years to gradually root in at the semi-leisurely pace you are seeing now, it might still feel wrenching. However, we are talking about ten years, ten years for a major change of focus in almost every aspect of life; change that will affect everyone on deeply personal levels.

The chain of factors causing such a quick shift are an ecologically overspent, in-debt world, in recession, all of which you have already. Add increasingly strong and erratic weather, falling food-production, increased volcanic activity and debris, a couple of devastating earthquakes in economically prominent areas and the globe will be reeling. The good news is that people will then be forced into using their creativity and into acting more locally, more collectively and more helpfully towards each other, simply because those are the only behaviors that have any chance of making life better.

Underlying these changes is an earth that must decrease human populations in order to heal and cleanse itself. These major shifts in consciousness are tremendously exciting times in any planet's history and many, many, many of you wanted to be around for the experience. However, it is not possible for all humans to remain and to keep breeding—even at less than the current exponential rates. Earth's population will most probably be reduced by 20-percent by the year 2000. More on that later, but you are right, it is not going to be easy; there is much human grieving to do over the loss of perhaps one billion people.

CHAPTER 3

Soul Age Concepts
Reincarnation Revisited

*The human race, to which so many of my readers belong,
has been playing at children's games from the beginning,
and will probably do it till the end, which is a nuisance for
the few people who grow up.*
—*G.K. Chesterton*

*The mark of the immature man is that he wants to die
nobly for a cause, while the mark of the mature man is
that he wants to live humbly for one.*
—*Wilhelm Stekel*

JOE AVERAGE IS HEARING VOICES

People make up the planet. The planet's basic feel depends on who is on it, how new and fresh, how old and wise or
just plain adventuresome. In earliest lifetimes, people focus on
survival issues; later, on developing order; much later, on developing personal power; then come the tasks of developing heart

and, finally, a personal spiritual philosophy which helps make sense of this rough old planet.[1]

At the present time on Earth, the average person, the person who is most mainstream, has already completed many lifetimes devoted to cultivating individualistic, materialistic and even quite aggressive behaviors, searching out his own advantage. Now Joe Average is coming out the other end of that experience, wondering if there isn't something more; life seems a little flat. Being on top, getting more, even having it all ultimately leaves a bewildering, lonely spot, which starts calling increasing attention to itself. The little voice is now getting louder and louder. Materialism doesn't feel quite so satisfying: looking only to one's own advantage simply doesn't have the same allure as previously. This is the hinge point at which many, many people find themselves now, and it is what is creating the period of fast change the Earth has now embarked on.

PEOPLE TRANSITIONS

Before moving on to the economic, social and Earth changes expected during the coming years, it would be appropriate to focus on the concepts of soul development because so much is based on these simple, yet extensively useful ways of looking at human behavior.

Reincarnation, the view that the human soul takes many bodies in its search for experience and enlightenment, weaves itself in and out through the soul age concepts. If reincarnation does not make easy intellectual sense to you, or annoys because of a Judeo-Christian upbringing, you can, if you wish, simply let yourself be aware that people do in fact seem to exist at different levels of development and capability, for whatever

---

[1] Humans are the sentient, self-reflective species on the land and the subject of this book. Dolphins and whales, the sentient species of the water, follow exactly the same soul growth patterns—without the technology or written language of humans. Interestingly, humans generally aren't seen as sentient by cetaceans, but as slow (not telepathic) dense thinkers, who neither play nor create at high levels. Cetaceans widely believe that humans are so violent that they could not possibly be sentient.

reasons. And, you can notice the ways in which different cultures, or even just different communities in your area, are affected by the developmental levels of people making them up, differences which can't be well accounted for by education alone, or income, or religion.

In a body, it is quite natural to think of chronological age as being something of a guide to how "mature" a person is. It certainly is true that experiencing life over many decades is likely to increase the ability to handle it better. A 40 year old is less inclined to fly off the handle than someone half that age, the major factor being longer perspective. Also, it is a rare 40 year old who would even consider going back to 20 were it possible; the wisdom the years give is too strongly valued.

However, there is a disparity among people which is easy to notice, right? Not all 40 year olds are balanced characters. Some children are more mature and capable, whether age two or age sixteen, than their peers. Occasionally teenagers are much more together than their own parents. Why is it that some find life easier to handle than others, others who may have many more years of experience under their belts?

One level of the answer is that in a cosmic, metaphysical sense, people's souls develop over a period of time, over the corpses of many bodies. In the Western world, people generally don't think about living many lifetimes; even less do they have any concept that completing many lifetimes creates a greater level of wisdom than when life first started. [2] But this is what actually happens. The soul does develop and mature over many dozens of lifetimes of experience. Just as with body age, the older your soul gets the more capable you tend to become because of the inner wisdom that extra experience creates.

Part and parcel of the "being physical" game, even for the experienced soul, is coming into a body, each time innocently, without conscious memory of all that has gone before. It may

[2] Reincarnation originally played a minor part in Christian theory. It was deleted as a political gambit in the 4th Century at Constantinople.

even take decades to figure out what you "planned" to accomplish with your life. Nevertheless, your body, personality, psychology, abilities and talents, your degree of flexibility or rigidity as well as the richness or the flatness of your thinking are all influenced absolutely and powerfully by the number of lifetimes you've had and the growth and insights you have gained through all that experience. These traits or memories come in with your essence and energy field, not through your body's cellular structure. (Energy field patterns, though, do have a strong effect on your body, right down to its cells.)

FIVE DISTINCT SOUL SEASONS

There are five rather distinct levels or stages the soul goes through in its lengthy maturation process. Before your very first incarnation, all of you signed up for the whole game. The only way out is through, i.e. by completing the whole game.[3]

These five levels bring to mind the image of chronological body age, which is why we label them that way. The first developmental level we call *infant*, and it occurs in the earliest group of lifetimes. Like an actual infant, the person tends to feel very new and awkward in the body. Life is not known; it seems fairly scary and complicated. When, after many lifetimes, you perceive on an inner level that you have gained enough control over survival issues, you move along to the next growth stage and start exploring more of your world. The *baby* level is akin to being a toddler; you have gained more confidence, but are not yet independent, and despite some bluster you cling tightly to your parental code of conduct. When rules, order and dogma are examined, experienced and assimilated in all aspects, an individual then pushes off into the next level, *young*. Here, you hit your worldly stride and manage to get out there, use your will, get things done, make money and have impact. When that's complete, it is on to the emotional

---

3 There are always system-breakers, but Michael says jumping out of the system tends to happen because of the compounded stuckness of lifetimes, not quick enlightenment.

issues of life. The *mature* level tends to be able to handle most areas of life well, and gradually learns to handle emotion in all its aspects. At the last stage, *old*, you grow less enthralled by either emotion or worldly success. Instead, your struggle—and pleasure—will be to find clarity about the purpose of life, and a means of expression which is true to your heart, soul and self, and serves others or the Earth in a way that interests you.

To expect a baby soul to handle life like a mature soul is similar to expecting a ten year old to master psychology and become a therapist—at ten! You are pushing the process. Infant or baby souls will not respond in the way an old soul will, nor will they necessarily act logically or reasonably according to a mature soul's definition. It is for these reasons, and a myriad of others, that the soul ages tend to have a rough time trusting and understanding each other.

Each soul age stage is augmented by all previous experience, but proceeds off on its own trajectory. No level is any better or worse than any other—in fact, each has virtues and also causes its own brand of trouble, for itself and for others. Each of these five major levels of human unfoldment commonly takes 20 to 40 or 50 lifetimes to complete, depending primarily on whether a given essence likes moving speedily or at a leisurely pace. Those who enjoy moving fast often lead fairly disheveled physical plane existences; those who prefer life at a slower, more thorough pace tend to keep the material plane scene nicely together, but are prone to becoming stolid, stuck and mired—unlike the fast movers. Which is better? Neither, it simply depends on who is doing it and what kind of Earth experiences a soul wants to create. The world is a more interesting place because fast, slow, and middle-of-the-road exist.

Because the soul age information so strongly underpins coming world changes, it will be worthwhile to examine these concepts a bit more fully here.

THE INFANT SOUL

Infant lifetimes are the most rudimentary of times, with an individual's learning being predominantly centered around physical survival. Your intellectual center is not yet fully opened and you usually bump right into all the written and un-written rules of society. Not knowing what is expected, or how to fit in, makes for confusion and sometimes resentment. You are not confident. You don't easily understand what makes any-thing tick or what consequences your actions will provoke. Usually a fairly fearful individual who believes in the forces of spirits and possibly of demons, this soul age also lives with a sense of mystical oneness with nature simply because they are still so fresh from the Tao, from God,

Only a very small percentage of infant souls choose to live in complex Western societies, instead reasonably preferring simpler lives in more elementary cultures, with no checkbooks to balance, no electric bills to remember or pay, and no moral necessity to appear regularly each morning at 7:55 am to punch the old timeclock.

Earth is currently accepting its last few groups of new in-fant souls. This closure to new souls happens on most planets with sentient life and allows the average soul age of the planet to move forward more rapidly since it is no longer being con-tinually weighted by the entry of new souls.[4]

THE BABY SOUL

Graduate yourself to baby level and you hope that's it for huts and rudimentary living. This soul age sets out to acquire some polish—and, in fact, would feel proud about never being late to punch that timeclock. The goal of this phase is to de-velop and maintain order, internal and external, to the extent possible. This was the soul age that grouped together in Neolithic times and "invented" the civilizations we have just

---

[4] 5% infant in the U.S. and slightly less in industrialized Europe. Many undeveloped nations have 25–45% infant souls.

been discussing.

Nowadays, the baby soul often gets herself born into authoritarian societies, or migrates toward an authoritarian religion or a bureaucratic job to learn, and to begin to obey, the one "right" set of rules for socially acceptable behavior. A person in this good-citizen stage is happiest with you if you also obey the same rules, exactly to the letter, please. So, please keep that lawn mowed and go to church! The many baby souls in the U.S. are especially happy when ensconced in the clean, conservative, still stable, small- to medium-sized towns of middle America.[5]

THE YOUNG SOUL

The adventuresome young soul pulls away from the group-think of the baby period. These people do not want rules to restrict them and, if need be, will earn the right to become the rule-makers. Church here tends to be used as a place to network, not as a place to find "the rules" or a philosophy to help perfect one's behavior. Young souls want to be the quickest and the best and tend to have the tenacity and determination to mold life to their specifications.

The innate urge of the young soul period is to start building the ego and fulfilling it by putting an imprint on the world. At this third stage, the motto is, Might makes right. It doesn't matter whether the might is subtly implied power or blatant physical bullying; whatever gets the job done tends to be admired.[6] Because young soul energy flows easily after externals, they often climb towards the top of whatever field they choose. Smart, competitive, and hard-working, they have given the

---

[5] 20% in the U.S. The percentages vary widely in European countries, with baby souls generally making up the most traditional and conservative segments of any population. Societies with large traditional elements, like Germany, Spain, Portugal and Greece, have more, say 30-40%, and England, Holland, France, Sweden, 20% or less. Japan currently has about 35%.

[6] This explains the comment of one U.S. Senator who said the Russian coup failed because its leaders lacked the "courage" to kill Gorbachev and Yeltsin.

U.S. its competitive edge, its hi-tech marvels, and its recent roost at the top of the power heap. [7]

Prior to the mid-70s, young souls ruled a huge majority of countries. They still hold sway over nearly all third world countries, happily dictating how life is going to be in their domain. No, the responsibility does not make them nervous. It is the experience of power they are after, not making their part of the world cornucopic.

This young soul concentration of focus on the material plane develops stamina, backbone, individuality, courage, cleverness and leadership. It is not a stage which deals easily with emotion, or respectfully with the rights and feelings of others. In dealing with physical plane reality, the young soul is practical to a level difficult for the older soul to grasp.

THE MATURE SOUL

When the mature set of lifetimes begins, the drive towards outward success is mellowed by a new, often compelling desire to give personal, intimate relationships more time and importance. The work is now about developing a sense of connection with all life. The mature soul develops a conscience that can feel the impact of his actions on the world—impacts which rarely bothered the young soul at all. Some mature souls may feel so deeply connected with all life that it becomes too painful to drop bombs, subjugate people or even hunt for sport. If they abuse a child, or maybe just kick the cat, their conscience will throw guilt at them. Inner creativity, the feeling nature and people are what now matter.

Both the world and the U.S. have growing mature soul populations whose numbers are now greater than any other soul age. [8] Mature soul outlook has started to affect all the rest of

---

[7] 32% young world wide and in the U.S., where that percentage will continue to shrink. Japan, a smart new competitor has 40% young, with more on the way.

[8] The U.S. now has 33% mature; Europe, including Eastern Europe (excluding Albania, Bulgaria, Spain and Portugal) has between 30 to 45% mature.

society, exhibiting something of the famous hundredth monkey effect whereby consciousness changes slowly at first and then suddenly, like lightning, as more and more monkeys—or people—start acting in some particular fashion.

THE OLD SOUL

The last stage of earthly development, the old-soul phase, focuses a person's attention on a search for meaning and on finding a way to come into acceptance of life as it is. The growth lessons of this stage prompt a person to begin to detach from emotional drama and intensity and to de-emphasize material needs. The resultant philosophical detachment is often the basis of a rather keen sense of humor about life.

While old souls with so many lifetimes under their belts may be rich and wise internally, they aren't much valued in a materialistic, action-oriented world. Furthermore, it usually takes them until at least age 35 to coherently pull their many facets together, and that can be embarrassing. (Young souls are internally integrated by about age 20.) Figuring out how you want to express yourself in a world you're not particularly in tune with takes time also. As an old soul you are concentrating less attention on the material plane, so you are less likely to be well off financially, and thus incur another loss of status. For all these reasons, the old soul tends towards self-deprecation. On top of that, there is a strong tendency towards laziness: Yes, you have done it all before. But despite difficulties, the well pulled-together old soul has quick access to the very broadest of perspectives and an ability to stay centered and objective when others can't.[9]

Many old souls get sloppy and disrespectful in their dealings with the physical plane, which, or course, tends to make life less comfortable and less enjoyable. The idea is to

---

[9] The U.S. has 10% old souls overall, though they tend to concentrate themselves in cer - tain areas; Europe generally has between 10 and 15%, Holland and Iceland upwards of 20%; Japan has 5% .

be able to handle the material plane with ease, to put sufficient attention on it that life flows smoothly, which then allows you to pursue spiritual and philosophical interests. It would be very rare and odd to graduate yourself from life on the planet until you can handle it with grace and can find sustained enjoyment and pleasure in physical existence.

HOW SOUL AGE FLAVORS A NATION

You can see right off how having an abundance of any one of these soul age groupings in a country will deeply affect what goes on within its borders—and sometimes without as well. Furthermore, as soul age mixtures change according to who is being born, a nation will change to reflect what is happening with its citizens. Many times countries will grow in a logical progression, just like a person, from infant to baby to young. That kind of growth tends to make a society feel more stable and comfortable as it changes. But interestingly and confusingly, a country can also be strongly young or mature and then fall back a notch or two to baby, if that is who decides to start being born there. Several Arab nations are in this situation currently, having more baby souls and fewer young, mature and old souls now than they did centuries ago. India and Persia were once favored old soul enclaves, but no more.

Previously we highlighted some of the more agreeable societies that have been created by baby souls coming together.. They have also created the not-so-kind; baby souls have instigated hundreds of holy wars to proselytize and force change on others; they have with regularity lynched, burned and tortured humans with different views; they have created and lived with extreme xenophobia, especially in the East; and, in all corners of the world, they have practiced bigotry against every other color and stripe of human. Noisy intolerance of differences among people is the major social shortcoming of baby souls.

When young souls incarnate, they aim to have power and

control. Their purpose is to see what they can then physically create. Feudalism, which often worked out to be a harsher system than slavery, was a political form tailor-made to give handfuls of young souls the experience they craved of power over others. In fact, the hierarchical governmental styles of the last 2-3000 years were enjoyed and perpetuated by the young soul, who usually managed to get himself born into the "right family" in the first place in order to insure his piece of the action. (Without a favorable birth, a man would pick up the nearest available power tool, perhaps a sword to fight his way in, an education, a skill, or a wife with a rich father. A woman traditionally needed to find a man to seek power through.)

Colonialism, yet another young soul invention, gave whole countries a chance to exploit wide areas of the world. Britain, France, Spain, Portugal, Belgium and the Netherlands all built themselves latter-day empires by subjecting militarily and technologically weaker nations to their whims and wills. The New World especially offered unprecedented opportunity—guns, horses, plus blankets loaded with the smallpox virus provided an easy victory against native populations. Some colonists were concerned about bringing their one true religion to the locals at the edges of the world, while others were concerned with bringing order or education, but the basic impetus was the plunder of foreign resources.

Huge standing armies, another young soul fantasy come true, can roll over neighboring territory with enough manpower to scare or scorch everything else off. Napoleon said he cared nothing for the lives of millions; neither did Hannibal, Alexander the Great, Attila the Hun, Genghis Khan, or Hitler. History is full of the names of these military giants with expansionistic dreams. Mature souls often fight with their neighbors over bitter, old issues, but they tend to lose capacity for the amount of violence required to keep empires under control.

Dictatorship, typically an egotistical, strong-armed way

to rule, is easier for a young soul to accomplish when the masses look to authority to tell them what to do. Baby and infant souls are innately suspicious of independent thinking; you don't have to twist their arms to get obedience. Tyranny is more difficult to pull off against a countryside of young souls—as Britain found out in Massachusetts. Mature souls will choose lifetimes under oppressive political systems to use the emotional intensity as a growth experience, though sometimes they also rebel. Old souls are generally so completely fed up with despots and disheartening political systems that they plan their lifetimes carefully to avoid both. However, they occasionally get stuck too. Political realities aren't all that predictable and sometimes don't come close to matching your astral plan. Talk to all those old souls in Russia about that!

THE YOUNG SOUL WORLD, PAST AND PRESENT

The Roman Empire straddled the baby/young borderland, both in its distribution of soul ages and also in its period of power. You found sturdy, grounded guys out tromping around, clashing with the common folk, raping and pillaging as the saying goes, but always pushing forward, grabbing territory as they went. To these territories they proudly brought their brand of civilization, structure and infrastructure. As the empire grew ever more colossal, clever new ways to keep it all running smoothly were invented. This wasn't simply about bleeding the outlying territories of money and resources, but about the pleasure and challenge of creating order and structure in the hinterlands, a sometime baby soul passion.

For the last several thousand years, the largest, most influential soul age group has been the young soul gang. Their numbers, which kept increasing as people evolved and populations increased, obviously had much to do with how history now reads. A few examples here, which get quite specific about how their influence worked, will make it possible to see more clearly what exactly the world is now turning from.

Individuals sitting atop the power heap will almost always fight change in order to protect personal privileges. When young souls begin being born poor in large numbers, something in society always has to give. When Europe started burgeoning with impoverished young souls, it became imperative to find an arena where their new energy and sense of themselves could be used. Enter North America! Because it was primarily the energetic, enterprising individual who managed to beat his way to the shores of North America in the first place, the young nation became, with the aid of these disenfranchised masses, a country with a strong young soul flavor. Young souls will jump faster than anyone to grab an opportunity to forge a better life, even if it means doing something so wrenching as leaving behind everything which is familiar.[10]

These adventuresome and desperate souls created a new kind of country, one based on the freedom of the individual (well, the white male anyhow) to excel, grow, do business and bear arms as he wished. Rustling the country away from its original caretakers with strong-arm tactics and double-dealing was predictable behavior for a gang of young souls. Notice, though, that the actions and tactics taken against the Indian nations were hugely more acceptable then than they would be at the present moment. The approach of the Columbus quincentenary focused the issue, and thinking changed tremendously

One reason why the U.S. became so powerful and successful was simply its young soul willingness to exploit resources, work hard, and keep a clever eye open for better, more efficient ways of doing things. The country which rushed to fulfill its "manifest destiny" had no qualms about draining less developed nations for profit, so long as those nations weren't

---

[10] Originally a penal colony, Australia's young soul underpinnings are quite similar. Because it was further from Europe and in the emptier Southern Hemisphere, it didn't have quite the same opportunity for industrial expansion or world dominance. The young soul urge towards unlimited personal freedom still runs high in Australia.

(exactly) colonies, an understandably touchy subject for the new and expanding nation.

That the country was strong and could do what it wanted was cause for much young soul relief and celebration, not self-examination or guilt. Though the U.S. controlled as much of the world as it could, the means and verbiage were more subtle than the colonial control methods of previous centuries; still, there was little worry over the propriety of displaying military might to protect investments abroad. Today, the huge U.S. military force and defense budget are widely seen as a potentially fatal drain on the country. For the young soul of the past, a potent military was imperative because it enhanced status and gave muscle to all interactions with the rest of the world. Traditionally the U.S. had two feet on the young soul side of the military equation; now, one foot is tentatively moving onto mature soul turf. Many more people are sensing that fighting has its drawbacks, even for the "winners". Projecting his dark side onto the Soviets, Reagan ordered up piles of weapons, picking the pockets of the middle class to do it and saddling the future with a $2.5 trillion deficit. Citizens who feel comfortable about letting the military corral nearly half the country's wealth each year are rarer and rarer. New solutions are begging to be found, though the timing is not yet quite ripe for the leaders to appear; the citizenry must first be solidly behind changes of this nature because backlash potential is high.[11]

These days, when a country has fresh gangs of young souls, like the Pacific Rim countries, Luxembourg and Monaco, putting a bunch of guys in military outfits and telling them to grab what they can won't work quite as beautifully. You might manage to expand a border or even soak up a country or two, but no more empires lie waiting to be formed with these tactics. It is brighter and more discerning to find another niche, which Japan, Singapore, South Korea, Luxembourg and Monaco

---

[11] John Kennedy's assassination was provoked because he was pulling away from militarism in Vietnam and Cuba, as Oliver Stone's film, JFK, suggested.

have done quite nicely.

Technology has always been helpful along the path to power. Swords and daggers, ships, tanks, telescopes, satellites, cannons and bombs all have been able to give one country or another an edge over others. Japan, after clear and humiliating defeat, saw the future wasn't war and quickly and dexterously retrenched and rebuilt, discovering in the process that technology itself could be a means to riches and world domination.

When technology blooms in a young soul country, it is often without much common sense or morality around it. It just goes where it goes, no holds barred. Imagine being in a vegetative coma (like nearly a million U.S. citizens) and being kept alive by a machine that insists on breathing for you, for five or ten years?[12] Or imagine being a scientist, sizing up the potentials of a sticky, volatile substance called napalm. Young souls are likely to be the ones to push ahead with something as tricky as nuclear weapons or genetic manipulation, experimenting with little concern for potential problems. If it can be done, like the atom bomb, the young soul wants to do it. (In fact, the young souls involved with that project had few of the moral repercussions that their mature soul co-workers did.) Those ecologically disastrous thirty-mile-long drift nets the Japanese insisted on "fishing" with, because they were so efficient (deadly), are another example of shortsighted technology, this time one that essentially sterilized the ocean and made tomorrow's catch ever more elusive.

GETTING YOURS IN A CHANGING WORLD

Young souls pretty much believe in getting theirs now, before someone else does. When they think at all about causing problems downstream, they tell themselves the people of the future will be clever and technologically advanced enough to figure out how to handle any difficulty that could arise. Their

12 You may not be spending much of your time in your body, but neither are you as free as you might be.

blindness to the need to shepherd and conserve resources is slightly disingenuous, as evidenced by their own greed to get at those resources, now, before someone else—and before they are gone.

The U.S. was originally set up with guaranteed freedoms and an egalitarian spirit so that the most ambitious could lead themselves to the top with everyone (well, those white males again) getting a fair shot at riches and political power. This made for a lot of competition which was thought of as good. Unlike traditional Europe or present-day Asia, Africa or South America, you could theoretically be born anywhere and with the required smarts, gumption and stamina aim for whatever heights your soul desired.

Currently, significant numbers of young souls are being born into the lower classes in several Latin American countries—like Brazil—where they rarely find a door to success they can pry open. In Latin countries, the children of the poor have ordinarily gone nowhere, but young souls have a very low tolerance for indentured servitude and lack of opportunity. They are migrating in hordes to Brazil's larger cities where, because jobs are not available, they are creating a major crime wave, driving the rich crazy. These poverty-stricken, ambition-charged souls are also pressing into the Amazon region to farm and mine. There they must contend with rich ranchers fighting a brutal fight to maintain their control of the area. These immigrants must now also contend with environmentally provoked policies making it illegal to burn the forest, typically their only route to land acquisition.

Like the 300 ragtag Ottoman nomads who rode into Constantinople and started an empire which spread out over seven centuries, young souls are adventurers who will nearly always take action to force the issue of their own success. Taking action may be as innocent as making sure you get the grades and loans for college; or it may be as difficult as forcing your own society to open its doors and rethink its policies. Brazil's upper crust is being pushed to find ways to accommodate its influx of young souls, a valuable resource it currently wastes.

When a young soul elite is running a country, it instinctively tends to keep the poor from being educated or too well fed; conscious or unconscious, the idea is to maintain tight control. Feeding the poor, educating them or letting them have a shred of hope, control or self-respect feels dangerous because soon these unwashed masses could be agitating for a bigger piece of the pie. Cruelly using people as fodder for your own wealth and comfort is part of the young soul experience, and part of what is changing as the world moves along.

The new consciousness permeating the globe says people count; it is not okay to treat any of them like subhuman dirt beneath your feet. (In fact, animals are due to get more rights in this period too.) Young souls needing to experiment with power and leadership will still get their experiences, but within more confined parameters in much of the world.

WATCH HOW THINGS CHANGE

Societies shift and evolve over time, the direction they take depending considerably on what soul ages are getting themselves born where. If the U.S. were suddenly to gain a larger contingent of baby souls (instead of the increase in mature souls), the country would become more conservative, protectionist and isolationist and would likely tread on several of the freedoms guaranteed by the Bill of Rights. Baby souls are more interested in running a tight, homogeneous ship than in freedom of thinking and action.

Germany, once the militaristic, young soul country that provoked two world wars, is now 35-percent each baby and mature, with only 20-percent young remaining. Mature souls easily understand baby souls and can help them mellow out their rougher tendencies. Reunification doesn't pose the traditional

threat since both baby and mature souls are family and community oriented—power politics now holds little interest.   In
fact, so many Germans found U.S. maneuvering in the Gulf war
embarrassing or reprehensible that they refused to pitch in the
money other nations did. Not surprisingly, the jobless, angry
youths of eastern Germany responsible for the resurgence of
Nazi emblems, social hatred and violence are generally young
souls.

India and Persia once were gentle, philosophical old soul
societies. Now, India is mostly baby, though moving at full
gallop towards a young soul phase. Persia became Iran, and
with Khomeini's revolution, most of its young and mature souls
managed to exit—with not a small amount of the country's
wealth and technical expertise. [13] The Dutch, notoriously cruel
colonists in their country's young soul phase, are now primarily
mature and old, utterly liberal, yet perfectly practical in their
politics and social policies. For centuries the young souls of
Latin America, who tended to congregate among the richest
ten-percent, easily held the reins on the impoverished baby and
infant soul masses. [14] Now, as mentioned, they are experiencing
a real threat to their rule from the sizable numbers of young
souls being born destitute into landless, jobless families.

In the post-war years, England moved away from its
colonial, young soul past and into a socialized, let's-take-care-
of-everybody configuration. Since the largest grouping of people there are now mature, the strong urge to dominate the world
is mostly just a memory, having been replaced by ideas about
social justice and fairness for all classes—except for the Irish.
Ethnic hostility is bound to increase and be a point of pain and
growth for many in a mature soul world. Mature souls rarely
blow up their planets—as young souls are prone to do when they

---

[13] Iran is now approximately 30% infant and 50% baby.

[14] Remember that every soul age feels freest and best when with its peers, meaning others
of the same soul age. Lifetimes are planned accordingly because this makes for optimal vali-
dation and the easiest growth.

have the technology—but they are famous for drama and wrenching fights with each other until their new-formed compassion is stretched to include even those annoying neighbors. Discord like this is not about an urge to dominate the world, but is more akin to the intense power struggles which often occur within families and long-term relationships.

Russia changed even more radically in those post war years than England. It moved away from heavy concentrations of baby souls, with aristocratic young soul domination, to become a primarily mature soul country with large contingents of old souls. These incarnating mature and old souls were aware that Russia was about to undertake an interesting, large-scale social experiment in which everyone was to give and take according to ability and need. These souls were unexpectedly faced with yet another group of ambitious young souls who quickly took control of the new power structure and ruled from their own needs and consciousness, until recently. Mikhail Gorbachev is a late mature soul with the rather large life task of putting those mature soul social experiments back on track. He is not likely to disappear from the world scene. [15]

As the planet ages, the people on the planet also age and develop. People make up societies and their stage of development is the major factor controlling the evolution their societies will make, or not make. With mature souls coming into more eminence, the qualities of life they naturally create will come more and more to the forefront of everyone's life, the primary qualities being caring interactions with people, animals and nature.

THE MATURE SOUL WORLD OF THE FUTURE

Right now, 700 out of every 1000 people are illiterate, 500 out of that 1000 will be hungry tonight and a mere 60 peo-

---

[15] Boris Yeltsin, an early mature soul, is a superb organizer and manager, both very helpful skills in fast changing times.

ple control half the money. Mature souls won't be able to put up with statistics like these for long because they truly want to live from the heart and can't help but feel connected to all humanity and concerned about fairness. Letting anyone starve or freeze or go without medical care or security in old age becomes anathema, for the underlying conviction is that all people should be taken care of—well, at least all of "us". The news is that the "us" keeps getting bigger and bigger.

Mature souls, of course, don't always pull off living openly from their hearts, and sometimes end up overwhelmed by emotionality caused by personal or political drama. But their lives and lessons are aimed towards being able to eventually accept all people into their hearts. When mature souls fight instead they may feel invigorated for a while, but soon it wears them out. Even victory, if it has meant stomping on others, doesn't feel clearly wonderful. The mature soul has many difficulties on the road to interdependence and cooperation, but that clearly is the chosen destination.

In the 90s, people will experience much amazement and some shock at how deep their interdependence runs. Borders have never been more porous, and not just to drugs or smuggling, but to ideas and diseases and the other guy's environmental dirt. What one nation decides clearly affects all. The iron fact of environmental interconnectedness will cause the foot-dragging U.S. and Japan to come under increasingly adamant world pressure to amend the practices which contribute to acid rain, dying oceans, dying forests, and ozone depletion. Before too many more years pass, the entire world will see the necessity of hashing out what to do about fossil fuel use.

MATURE SOULS IN THE U.S.

Mature souls in the U.S. have always been around, but never before with such high percentages. Collectively, they often formed the vocal minorities which took aim at societal injustice, often, like the abolitionists, agitating for those who had few rights. To a huge degree, they have been the creative phalanx, the constitution signers, writers, philosophers, artists, critics, satirists, scientists, actors, dancers, singers and musicians who made the country vibrant and rich.

The Roaring 20s gave the U.S. a highly noticeable group of mature souls. Given half a chance, this soul age will celebrate life to the maximum, and outlandish was the word for it. The 20s became party time, wild time, free-thinking time, a time to roll noisily over the straitlaced prohibitions of baby souls; giving them a few good shocks was part of the fun. Then came the years of the Great Depression, sobering enough to to put a lid on exuberant public displays of this new energy. Thus, the wilder aspects of this energy went underground in the hard times of the 30s, but social compassion was higher than ever and many political and social safeguards were put in place thanks to mature soul influence.

The next wild outbreak came in the 60s. The new, largish crop of mature souls were no longer willing to put up with dull gray, suited-up, three-piece, half-dead, nice 50s' housewife kind of lives. Once again, there was insistence on personal freedom, fun, emotional intensity, and more dope. Again the backlash reappeared, though this time the form was different. A president with exuberance and vision was murdered; civil rights leaders were killed and the economy of the 70s slipped badly— but none of this was enough to ruin the gumption or crush the values of this new crop of mature souls.

Though the gray world reasserted itself, this time much of what the hippies and the yippies were about got integrated into society. Life stayed a little looser. Peace and love and fun held infinitely greater appeal than another Vietnam.

Mature souls are once again asserting themselves in the U.S., in ever stronger, more prevailing ways. Anti-Gulf war demonstrators carried flags—instead of burning them—because they considered themselves to be a valid part of the culture. It is mature souls, mostly, who are working avidly to bring the still-powerful young soul corporate world to some common sense around the environment and ordinary citizens to some crisper thinking regarding throw-away consumption. Hunger and homelessness are both drawing strong attention, and so is a healthcare system that keeps few healthy. The educational system and the basic neglect of children in the U.S. will come into strong focus also; and fur-wearing, meat-eating, animal rights, victim rights, and the nearly continual stream of violence from television and movies. Mature souls will keep finding parts of life that need fixing and then throw their collective weight behind creating those changes.

Baby souls are the people who generally act as deadweight against change. Ridicule aimed by the media at the religious right and its rather gloriously failed leaders, Jerry Falwell, Jim Bakker, Oral Roberts and Jimmy Swaggart, have drained moral authority from that side, as did the hate-filled 92 Republican convention. Many of the righteous old sticklers of the far right have lost their seats in Washington and in state capitols. Political issues now easily controlled by baby souls are few, their territory slipping: They have been reduced to fighting over abortion rights, which they are doing with vigor, government support of the arts, which isn't terribly arousing, and trying to keep homosexuals from obtaining full civil rights.

THE WORLD NOW

Only in the last four years have mature souls bulged the bell curve in their direction. Worldwide, as in the U.S., mature souls now account for 33-percent of the population and young souls 32-percent. A single percentage point would not make such a tremendous difference were not the current of consciousness swerving so dynamically towards a mature soul world, a world where people count. For many right now, the effect is like getting magnetized forward by the future, sucked into it, ready or not.

Look at the events of the last year or two. The European Community countries carefully started cutting red tape between their borders, heading towards a similarity of laws. This difficult-to-achieve cooperation makes Europe incalculably richer. When the moment arrived that Eastern Europeans no longer had to put up with tyranny, they seized it and shook off their handful of dictators; even wretched Albania's citizens are occasionally stirring. Twenty or more areas in the old Soviet Union have declared themselves to be sovereign states desirous of self-determination. It is clear to most of them that they had best cooperate and compromise with each other—or risk devastation. (Occasionally, though, the fight looks too satisfying to resist; lessons then pile on lessons.) Nepal's revered but knavish and corrupt monarchy was attacked, again and again, until it agreed to make enough democratic reforms to satisfy the agitators. Dismantling apartheid is fiendishly difficult, but South Africa is plunging ahead, knowing finally that it must be done. Mature souls insist their societies be flexible.

The previously unthinkable is happening in nearly every corner of the world. Though not all uprisings or elections are successful—China, Burma, Haiti, Yugoslavia and more than a few African fiascoes come to mind—people are suddenly less willing to put up with the same old plagued existences. The increasingly large numbers of mature souls on the planet are managing to change the societies in which they live—and to focus world attention on others.

In the U.S., the mature soul viewpoint had enough critical mass that the military did not jump all over Saddam Hussein, first blush—nor did most Americans think it should have. It waited for diplomacy first. The mature soul forte in crisis solution is talk, talk and more talk, with everyone putting all their feelings and concerns on the table, aiming for solutions all can live with. The monumentally stubborn Hussein proved intractable. A young soul on a power trip like this may only understand a powerful fist coming back at him, a kind of military shock therapy. Even though flexing military muscle is going out of style, it will still be the only way some leaders hear no. In Hussein's case, it may take a bigger blow than the Gulf episode proved to be.

Though George Bush managed to attach glory to himself after the Gulf war, it left a funny after-taste and the glory proved to be short-lived. People are focused on economic and social issues and won't be distracted by the call to patriotism or the possibility of greater world domination. Life at home has to work and work well first. That's mature soul thinking.

THE SOUL AGES

Age	Person	Culture
Infant	Awkward, New Unsophisticated Unclear about Consequences Undeveloped Conscience	Simple Lives Nomadic, Tribal Connected with Nature Few Artifacts
Baby	Develops & Follows Rules Respects Leaders & Experts Conventional Rigid, Intolerant	Invented Civilization Family Centered Stable Communities Patriotic, Jingoistic
Young	Ambitious, Competitive Capable, Hardworking Efficient, Non-Emotional Self-Seeking, Shortsighted	Military Might, Wars Technological Wizardry Rich, Materialistic Conquers Nature
Mature	Creative Emotionally Open Desires Meaning & Beauty Soap Opera Drama	Cooperative, Egalitarian Creativity High Nature is Conserved Ethnic Fighting
Old	Relaxed Individualists Spiritual, Philosophical Focused Inward & Upward Lazy, Loose with Rules	Liberal, Non-Judgmental Solves Problems Uniquely Lives with Nature Infrastructure Shabby

CHAPTER 4

Environment and Population
Moral and Political Issues

What have they done to the Earth?
What have they done to our fair sister:
Ravaged and plundered and ripped her and bit her,
Struck her with knives in the side of the dawn,
And tied her with fences and dragged her down.
—Jim Morrison

Reminds me of my safari in Africa. Somebody forgot the
corkscrew and for several days we had to live on nothing
but food and water.
—W.C. Fields

THOSE YOUNG SOULS

The severity of the ecological situation has two major causative factors: one is long-time young soul control of the world; the other is burgeoning populations. With an orientation towards the natural world which could not be called respectful, young souls started taking dominion over the Earth several thousand years ago. Because their natural urge to use and exploit is strong they tend to blind themselves to down-the-road problems. Even now, as the very systems that support all life are collapsing, young soul consciousness (out-picturing as the politician, the corporate decision-maker, or the person who feels he's got to have more, come hell or high water) strives to deny the facts. But then nobody likes to be hit in the pocketbook, especially in a profit-motive world.

While it is normal for young souls to be looking towards their own immediate advantage, they can be wrestled down at this historical hinge point and pushed towards more appropriate, planet-regarding ways of operating. If you want mass survival, there are not many options here. Once mature soul consciousness gets a stronger grip and people see clearly that increased fulfillment does not come from increasing consumption, life will be different. Suddenly there will be a different feel to making the same "hard" (i.e. ecologically sane) decisions. People will be acting more collectively, watching out for each other and the planet. Humans everywhere will band together to keep business and political interests from allowing the Earth to slip past the point of no return. In the meantime, the large wave of virtually obsessed young souls desperately trying to get in their last licks at any cost will continue to play havoc with the growing necessity of handling environmental issues with integrity.

THOSE EXPLODING NUMBERS

While narrowness of vision is one root cause of planetary degradation, the other is burgeoning population. If the population explosion isn't confronted, other problems will continue to explode. Developed countries have too many over-consuming people; third world countries too many under-fed people and too little land to do anything about it. The environment copes with neither easily.

As a result of climbing populations, developed areas are

suffering from disappearing forests, wild lands and soil, severe air pollution, mountains of garbage, plenty of it toxic, filthy water, vanishing fish, gridlock and escalating crime. Developed countries also siphon off resources from the third world.

The third world has its gridlock too, not just from cars but from motorcycles, bicycles, donkeys, carts and people, people, people. The surge in people carried with it a surge in the rats, insects, bacteria and diseases that prey on humans; it has meant losing forests and rivers and soil, creating desert, and air and water pollution more severe than most industrialized first world countries. It now means having too little agricultural land to go around; if coffee, tea, cocoa, sugar and tobacco were immediately uprooted, and the land given over to the production of real food for local consumption (and even if soils and climates weren't deteriorating rapidly), most of these poor nations still wouldn't be able to nurture their swollen human populations.

From our perspective, it is clear that nearly six billion people exceeds the carrying capacity of the Earth—if you want a healthy planet and humans with healthy futures. Even if the world were sensibly and fairly run, a human population in excess of four billion severely pushes the limits of systems and resources. Not even at the height of Atlantean times was the planet's population so high, and never again is it likely to be.

On an essence level, you know that current population levels are unsustainable. One reason they are so inflated is that everybody wanted to be around for this transition: to observe, participate in and perhaps even direct the way it will go. And remember, babies don't happen simply because of the joining of sperms and eggs, but because souls are pressing to become physical. Although you with the physical bodies are actually in charge and it is your place to say, "Yes, please!" or "Not yet!" or "No way!", an essence wanting to become physical has the power to push people, and biology, around.[1] (It won't surprise some of you parents to hear this!) When millions of souls want bodies, there are more apt to be millions of new humans born.

And, many of you jumped into this dynamic time fully aware you might not be lingering through to a ripe old age. We are seeing a probable 20-percent drop in population over the decade, (interestingly enough) provoked by people-caused environmental degradation. However, even a drop of one billion in worldwide population won't "fix" the current environmental skid, though it will give the Earth a bit more breathing room, slow down the damage, and courteously give people a chance to rethink priorities and heal their natural world.

CLOSE TO THE EDGE

Each person on the planet knows, at least on an inner essence level, that this is a hinge period, life on the cutting edge. The fairly stable preceding decades which supported this big-time population growth are now jolting towards some kind of finale, maybe grand, maybe not. From the astral, your essence plans all kinds of growthful, exciting lifetimes that put your personality, once you see the picture, in shock.[2] Personality becomes attached to the body in order to play out the physical "game". Nearly always it has, shall we say, mixed feelings about leaving a body and letting go of life. And 20-percent have that on the agenda.

On both counts then, attitude and population, the Earth will be the recipient of some much needed help. Ecological systems are so quickly and dangerously weakening that without this rollback in human numbers and a concomitant shift towards re-

---

[1] Michael's viewpoint, as spoken by T.E. Lawrence: "Isn't it true that the fault of the birth rests somewhat on the child? I believe it's we who led our parents on to bear us and it's our own unborn children who make our flesh itch."

[2] The astral is the plane closest to the physical plane. When your body dies, more of "you" lights up on the astral plane, where you heal yourself from the pain of physical life, grow in emotional understanding and plan future lifetimes with your family of friends.

sponsible living, there was little chance for mass survival very far into the next century. Even with major consciousness and behavioral changes and declining numbers, the continued ability of humans to live at ease on the planet is still not guaranteed.

That is yet another reason so many of you are incarnate. "Can we make it? How close to the edge can we get?" We hear this from you! And, either you manage to get organized or you get to see how threatened and sparse life can become. Humans create the future by design or by default.

THE CASE OF DISAPPEARING DIRT

Loss of soil is one of the problems we see as most threatening to continued life on Earth. Chancy levels of soil loss are occurring in the third world and in the first world, chancy because topsoil doesn't come back. Good soils take a hundred thousand to a million years to build. Loamy, dark and beautifully fertile, they maintain moisture between rains and produce abundant, healthy crops. However, these soils have been so poorly husbanded that in the U.S. something like five tons *per person* are lost *every year*, blown and washed away. City people, even one generation away from the land, have difficulty grasping the importance of dirt. Good soils are the backbone of North American affluence; they produce the steady supply of affordable food on your table. Like other resources, soils are being depleted at a much greater rate than renewal can occur. Oil and coal, also non-renewable and on their way out, will eventually be replaced by better, cleaner energy sources, but what do you replace dirt with? World-wide greenhouse hydroponics?

U.S. soils have already lost nearly half their organic material and minerals and furthermore are full of the toxic residues of "modern" agriculture, residues which destroy microbial life. Let this worsen further and you have sterile soil, soil which won't support life. With good stewardship the organic and mineral content can be slowly rebuilt, but five tons per person of blown-away, run-off topsoil is lost, gone forever each year. It can't be rebuilt and there is no place from which to truck it in. Fertilizers or compost are not substitutes for soil. There is nothing to do, no fix but more time than you have. Agribusiness and short-term economics replaced the practical family farmers who did their best by the land. Now the land itself is disappearing.

Salty soil is showing up in all areas of the world which have been subject to chemicals and heavy irrigation. Irrigation water is not draining through the soil, so salts are building up in the soil and in the ground water below. Most plants abhor salty soil, they won't grow in it. This leads to further desertification. The solution? Quit chemicals—fertilizers, pesticides and herbicides. Restore the health of those soils, add minerals, add organic material, grow cover crops and appeal to the nature spirits or devas. Also replant forests, for even those hundreds of miles away help create more rain and deeper drainage. What is being done? Nothing of the kind. Bizarre technological "fixes" are being considered, young soul mechanistic science aiming to trick nature into a few more years of production.

Soil erosion is also a third world problem. Even the best of tropical soils won't support the intense agriculture being asked of them now, so they too are disappearing at alarming rates. As human populations boom, many marginal lands, including recently deforested areas, have been taken over by people trying to grow food to sustain themselves. Forests are now cut that used to help create regional rain. Less rain in these trickier climates can quickly equal drought, then famine. When tropical soils are abused by agriculture, for even just a couple of years, the soil stops supporting life, sometimes becoming unable even to create cover for itself. When nothing can grow, the dust storms are soon fierce. Then it is said, helplessly, The desert is encroaching. Human activity causes deserts; deserts then tend to self-perpetuate and grow.

The problems with soil aren't yet showing up strongly in

Western consciousness. But, as the climate becomes less benign in the U.S., the marginalization of once good soils will play to a larger, more concerned audience. Poor soil quality will then be seen as tightly related to poor crop years and the shortage of food.

TREES

Vital to the continuation of life on Earth, trees make the atmosphere breathable—and they make the Earth beautiful. They help make rain, they manage water, soften the weather, and they make food and shelter for myriad creatures. Trees are disappearing too, and not just from excess logging and development. They are dying everywhere, on their own, weakened by the modern world.

Trees have a lot going against their continuation. They are valuable for paper, for fuel and to build things with, so people cut them. They also cover land that developers, road builders or farmers want, and more are cut. Many species are so sensitive to polluted air that they weaken and die, like in the mountains around Los Angeles. Trees also find themselves growing in forests previously clear-cut, perhaps several times, where the soil has eroded and lost vitality. So the trees aren't as vital and more easily succumb to diseases. Acid rain is hard on trees too, just as it is on the finish of your car. It kills them though. While trees can often survive the summer's extra heat or lack of precipitation, they are weakened and after a while can't fight off the insects or a new fungus going around.

Forests around the world are under stress and dying. The world's oldest standing forests are being rapidly chopped away. This situation is critical: Humans aren't technological enough to live without them. Plant trees, nurture trees and protect them. It will make a difference.

WATER LOSS

Water loss is another severe problem. Aquifers, the huge underground chambers that have gathered water into them over millions of years, once seemed inexhaustible. Worldwide, people are pumping this fossil water at much greater rates than it is replaced. Half the wells in Beijing are dry, with the water table dropping six or seven feet a year. Mexico City, still growing by a million a year, is now losing eleven feet annually from its aquifer. In India, old, always productive wells must now be dug deeper, or the village loses its water; many can't be dug deep enough to find year-round flows. In Arizona, it is often illegal to dig a well because the water table has sunk too drastically to allow unmetered use.

Because of deforestation, less and less water soaks into the ground and into the aquifers each year. Fewer trees also mean less water evaporating into local clouds and less local rain. What rainfall there is quickly runs off into streams and oceans (taking plenty of topsoil with it) instead of soaking in and enhancing groundwater. Water is simply not as available as it was five years ago, much less 20 years ago, or 100. This resource is more literally being "drained away" than others also in short supply.

People and their lawns, landscaping, agricultural and sewage needs have simply outstripped the amount of water available. Fossil water is near exhaustion and the skies don't rain as much. What do you do for encores? Young souls say desalinate, dam everything and colonize Mars if necessary. The world, though, is learning there are limits to rerouting and damming rivers if you don't wish to put local ecological systems in havoc.

Severe water shortages will continue to appear, making life less plush in all parts of the globe. Shortfalls of water can mean shortfalls of food—not just a quick, low-flow shower. Water is important enough that wars can start over it. Many countries now share water more or less peacefully, but what happens when water is less abundant? Or what happens to Israel, for example, which now takes nearly half its water from an aquifer under the West Bank, if it is pressured by the world to give the West Bank back? What happens anyhow when that aquifer is drained? Fiery flare ups provoked by water issues are especially probable by the mid-90s in the Middle East.

What water there is is increasingly polluted—bad for people, worse for children, hell for fish, and more often than you might imagine, so bad even industry cannot use it. Pollution of fresh water is a simpler problem than lack of water. You stop putting garbage, sewage and chemicals in it. After a while it is better; the river or stream or lake begins to heal—unless it is being made acid by airborne forms of pollution. Sane, ecological solutions appear to cost businesses and cities a great deal of money, so they come slowly, with much foot-dragging. In reality, these changes cost nothing compared to the cost of dragging your feet in this moment of time. The future needs to be preserved.

ATMOSPHERIC GASES

People worry when they notice unprecedented heat waves, snows, droughts and storms stacking up. The problems caused by the Earth's changing blend of atmospheric gases are currently receiving the most attention and rightfully so. Ozone depletion and greenhouse effects overshadow all other ecological problems by creating sudden and dramatic jumps in the magnitude of storms, temperature extremes, and in the case of ozone depletion a vast general breakdown in biological immunity—meaning your immune system isn't so good and neither is the tree's.

Because of people, industry, cows, and new chemical compounds, the atmosphere's composition has changed, and continues to change. In turn, the Earth is changing because its heat can't as easily get out. The young soul mentality waits, somewhat deviously, for all those greenhouse predictions to prove irrevocably true before making consequential changes in the business-as-usual machine, just as George Bush waited for the ozone hole to form over the Northern Hemisphere, his hemisphere, before talking substantive action.

Europe, Canada and even the occasional Latin country are doing better, making commitments and taking action with the intention of creating solutions. The U.S. and Japan have been the fiddlers, making do with whitewashes, greenwashes, more studies and obfuscation. Standoffs between those working to protect personal and environmental health and those seeking to protect business and jobs will be a continuing source of tension until near the end of the decade, when the obvious dependence of humans on a healthy biosphere makes it too scary to muck around any further.

When you are serious about fixing the environment, the will to take the profit out of polluting and out of consuming finite resources will be found. Then, the cost of environmental damage will start being fully factored into public decision making and the cost of lost resources or pollution will be reflected in the price of goods. This is called green thinking and green taxation.

When the world's heat gets trapped by these greenhouse gases, what happens? Weird weather. The pattern of change, as you well know, is rarely smooth and uniform. Overall you will have fiercer summers and winters and more erratic springs and falls; more fires, avalanches and tornadoes; more difficulty growing crops, except in a few lucky places; warmer tropical oceans, dying coral, dying fish, dying sea mammals, plus monster water-borne hurricanes, typhoons and cyclones; rain in deluges, or dearth, with erratic annual patterns; and trees under yet more stress. These, then, are the weather patterns and events we see as likely based on continued high releases of greenhouse gases. To these you may add the temporary cooling effects of increased volcanic activity.

STRATOSPHERIC GASES

High up and very thin, the stratosphere has had a roughly constant amount of ozone layered in it. Life formed on Earth while this layer conveniently protected plants and creatures from what would have been harmful amounts of the sun's ultraviolet rays. Now the composition of the stratosphere is changing; human activity has chlorinated it, thereby destroying ozone and creating ever widening gaps in this protective layer. Chlorofluorocarbons or CFCs, the chemicals at fault, are on their way out, but still widely used in spray cans, refrigerators, air conditioners, plastic foams and in cleaning microchips.

Major volcanic outbursts also reach up to the stratosphere, literally blowing holes through the ozone layer; these holes traditionally last for a couple of years before knitting back together. All that extra chlorine up there now from CFC usage changes the picture considerably because it mixes with volcanic sulfuric acid and ever more potently knocks down ozone, creating bigger, more dangerous permanent holes. The sharp rise we expect in volcanic activity over the next ten years is horrible news for the ozone layer and the protection it gives most life.

The problems connected with ozone destruction should be sobering, skin cancer being probably the least perilous of them. Phytoplankton instinctively retreat from extra ultraviolet by going deeper into the ocean; there they get less light, but then can fix less carbon—so you get more greenhouse gases and potential heat. As one-celled plants, plankton will be able to adapt to some degree, but because they are at the heart of the oceanic food chain, the entire ecosystem will weaken as they weaken. Plants, trees, and most food crops are also hurt by ultraviolet radiation. This unfortunately means less green life overall, more greenhouse heat and worsening famines. People, animals and plants will find their immune systems weakened by this extra ultraviolet radiation; immune system degradation will be a major contributing factor to the impending worldwide decline in population.

UV radiation eventually clouds the crystalline lens of the eye. Australians already are being strongly warned to protect their eyes from this potential, though when humans get cataracts these days it is a simple procedure to replace the clouded lens with an artificial one that works fairly well. Animals and insects, unless they are nocturnal, will have all day long, every-day exposure without the protection of sun hats and sunglasses or the saving grace of lens "replacements". Large-scale blindness would wreak havoc on the entire animal kingdom.

It has been fifteen years since the warning sounded. Because damage by these CFC chemicals is so straightforward and so nightmarish, it should have been possible to get rid of them fast. It is much simpler, after all, to root them out of industry than to retool the internal combustion machine or to leave forests alone. Though the aerosol and foam packaging trades have made positive changes, most CFC industries in the U.S. haven't yet been jolted into green public relations, much less total cleanups. Many countries, usually the mature soul ones, saw the danger from these chemicals as so extreme that they unilaterally began phasing them out, without the support of the U.S. It seemed the moral and prudent thing to do. It will take a global commitment to handle this one, and even then the turnaround time before the stratosphere could possibly start recovering and improving would be a long seven years, and probably twice that.

WEATHER NO LONGER DEFAULT CONVERSATION

The sun, which goes through cycles, looks as if it will be getting stronger and hotter over the next 15 or 20 years. With that brightening sun, the greenhouse gases already in place, and the many (unfavorable) feedback loops which tend to keep the fires fed, the world is due for more violent and extreme weather as normal weather patterns fall apart. While the greenhouse gases are in place and coming on strong, it is not yet clear how much overall heating will be created in the 90s. Volcanoes will have their temporary cooling effects. Beyond weather being violent, unpredictable and hard on humans (and animals, insects and plants), it is not easy to tell whether the next ten years will actually bring on much extra heating. It is a unique, complicated, grab-bag situation the planet is in. Weirdly, these greenhouse gases could bring cooling instead if the newly hotter oceans and air end up creating more high cloud cover. Right now, what is clear is the lack of balance or normal patterning. If the 90s get past the volcanoes and heat up, it won't be by a large amount nor will it cause a significant rise in the seas. If ecological sanity is not found (i.e. the greenhouse gases carbon dioxide, methane, CFCs and nitrous oxides continue to be released), then the early 2000s will be rougher weather-wise than the current decade, and hotter.

If people and industry don't confront their habits and massively reduce the release of greenhouse gases into the atmosphere, and plant trees as if they alone could save the world, we notice a very interesting, worst-case scenario developing. What we are seeing, by about 2030 on current trends, is the potential meltdown of the polar ice in the Arctic, without an equal, corresponding Antarctic melt. As you might imagine, polar asymmetry would play havoc with weather patterns. But even more startling, it appears that the planet would soon wobble and shift on its axis as an adjustment to its newly bulging oceanic equators and the odd unipolar weight pattern.

A prior (asteroid induced) axis shift flash-froze those famous woolly mammoths while they were peacefully grazing on springtime buttercups. Not a pleasant prospect for humans, and not much of a probability at this point. But that probability (currently less than 20-percent) will grow over time if the basic inputs from human activities are not radically altered.

MORALITY AND RESPONSIBILITY
The U.S. has yet to see the wisdom of becoming energy

efficient.   Reagan lowered the miles-per-gallon standards for new cars with hardly a squawk from the public.   Then he dismantled alternative energy research (and Jimmy Carter's solar panels on the White House roof).   As an oilman, President Bush saw many more reasons to drill in the fragile Arctic than to change the type of light bulbs used in government offices (which would save an equal amount of energy).   Though most Western European countries, and also Japan, are far ahead of the U.S. in energy efficiency, this issue gets little attention from the media either. When awareness comes and pressure is applied, watch out! Energy efficiency is an area ripe for quick, positive results.   When people are ready to deal with these issues, they will start turning bad situations and sloppy thinking around.

The older the average soul age in a nation, the more likely it is to concern itself over the whole.   The U.S., for example, has not taken what you could call the high moral ground, being more inclined to stall meaningful change than to create it.   With a sluggish economy, Bush and other business-first leaders found it simple to ease up on environmental regulations because people were more fearful about job security than about world ecological security.   But had Bush gained the wisdom to push for an environmental turnaround, many individuals, not just corporations, would have fought hard against it, while Europeans have, in contrast, pushed their governments into integrity and action.

For an example of what people-power can do when the timing is right, look at what happened with the nuclear dilemma. In the 70s and 80s, the probability of nuclear annihilation was much higher than it is currently. What happened? A few people (mostly mature souls, principally women) started moving with commitment and power to change the scenario, and to release the planet from the young soul male fantasies which could have easily pushed the button on global thermonuclear war. As more and more people joined in, future scenarios started to shift. This was no small thing. Making it through the young soul period without a fatal, self-inflicted wound was predictably tricky on a planet as aggressive and technological as Earth.

When enough of the general populace finds the same intent to fix the environment, an immense amount of attention will be focused on straightening out laws, taxes, lifestyles and technology. Politicians and industry will have no choice but to get real and get moving. The environment is, of course, a thousand times more complicated and difficult to repair than nuclear annihilation was to avert.

NATIONAL SUICIDE

There are many, many places in the third world where malnourished populations barely manage to sustain themselves. One way they survive is by essentially committing national suicide with remaining natural resources. Population pressures are pushing people into encroaching on traditionally wild areas. There aren't a lot of options, but as the forest is used up for fuel or timber, or the last bird or bear or monkey killed, or fish poisoned from mining run-off, the noose around everybody's neck tightens. Always the local populations feel it first. These men and women are not exploiting their country's resources to make a profit from teak office furniture, ivory bracelets or cheap hamburgers, but simply for their own survival needs. Unfortunately, the resources don't come back and fewer and fewer people can be supported year to year.

Many times there are simple, ingenious solutions which can help shift these seemingly impossible situations so that wild areas can be saved while people find a new way to provide for themselves. As the decade moves on and third world governments become more accountable for their actions, we expect more individual activity on these levels and more peace corps type activity too. The ideas and money to support change must usually come from outside, from people or groups dedicated to finding remedies for apparently hopeless, painted-into-the-corner situations. The poor don't usually have the overviews or knowledge to be able to jump outside their survival frame of reference and dream up solutions; the third world elite, who enjoy the fruits of the present system, won't usually pitch in money, especially if the poor will in any way become empowered.

Myriad multinational corporations have their hooks into the resources of undeveloped countries, often with very little benefit to the locals, mostly loss. That kind of activity, like the deals which send old growth Oregon forests to Japan to be processed into woodchips, is an undertaking of a whole different order. It is about convenience and short-term profit. While Oregon loggers may fear the survival of their way of life, they are not facing malnourishment and death, which is what the third world person may face. The onus of responsibility is greater on the first world because there are many more options, more freedom of choice, and usually more education and consciousness.

IF YOU'VE SEEN ONE REDWOOD TREE...

Earth will, with high certainty, continue to be the place humans call home. People will stick with Earth, bearing the many debts of mismanagement. Dolphins and whales, though, are gradually being "seeded" onto a planet of their own because, through no fault of their own, the oceanic environment, their environment, is no longer healthy or life-supporting. The aim of all those suicide beachings is to demonstrate how intolerable the oceans have become; they are emotional pleas for humans to expand their consciousness and change their behaviors. From the standpoint of the whole universe, the two most uncivilized behaviors possible for a sentient species are one, blowing up or otherwise poisoning your planet past the point of habitation; and two, harming other sentient species. Earth is consequently viewed as a wild, uncivilized place it's best to be wary of.

What is not yet clear is how much more austere and empty of life the Earth will become. New consciousness is growing, but it is not yet dynamic enough to turn events toward the most favorable of possible outcomes. A tilt towards cleaning up exists, but the will is not yet sturdy enough to actually make the deeper adjustments necessary for ecological systems to regain health. Is the planet going to find new balance or crash further into chaos—and eventual austerity? Humans have abundant free will to work with on that one.[3]

Even though you are witnessing the passing of the young soul phase and are clear that the currently embedded materialistic way of life is dysfunctional, changing your lifestyle for a dream, an ideal, or a question mark is never a popular mass activity. People do not like to give up anything they have gotten used to, whether it's Roundup on the front lawn, slaves to work and cower for you, fossil fuels, cows, or blowing smoke into the communal air. Only a few choose to live more simply or more ecologically because they have been rationally or morally swayed to do so. Usually, there has to be a shock, a catalyst which makes change unavoidable and creates a broad-based desire to get moving. Then your politicians act or get pushed out.

Bundled right up with these impending environmental and economic difficulties is a humbler way of life. When spurred by events many of you will see the future and choose to feel good about simpler lifestyles and happy about elementary things like not putting your car's weight of carbon dioxide into the atmosphere each year. Others (of you?) will be kicking and screaming, regretting the loss of material goods to changed circumstances and new policies. While there will be bright sides to reorganizing your world, feeling forced to give things up, forced to make change never feels good—even when you are convinced there must be a silver lining in there, somewhere.

By making more group and local, community-level decisions, people will ultimately feel more in control of their lives.

---

3 You always have free will, though your essence often pulls for a different experience than your personality would ever choose. What appears to be a poor choice to your personality often yields much of interest, speedy growth and the completion of old karma.

While life may seem harder without as many gadgets, luxuries, imports, meat meals or whatever, the sense is that Earth has at least received some time to heal and push the debris of the 20th century out of its body. Respect for the fragile threads of life, for the planet and its creatures with their myriad interconnections becomes almost a new religion. And, in fact, there is a new way of thinking, feeling and being emerging. The everyday world feels more sacred. You understand that as you simplify your life the world is healing, becoming a healthier place. Freshly in tune with nature and grateful for the good that they do receive, many people will come into a deeper, more profoundly sensed connection with the Earth.

THE AVERAGE PLANET?

One occurrence that regularly shows up at the end of a young soul era, on a majority of planets, is environmental degradation. You can see that Earth is right on schedule! The reason for this pattern is that any sentient being will be most out of touch with the needs of the planet which supports them during the young soul era. Once mature souls start gaining control, the issues get clear: Will the environment continue to be degraded without much thought? Or, does the alarm sound and the situation turn around? These are always big questions.

The turn to mature consciousness means environmental awareness will be growing, but the eventual state of any planet depends on how fast problems are tackled after the young souls have had their turn. Does the sentient species sit on its collective hands or tails, or does it manage quick policy changes?

"If you've seen one redwood tree, you've seen them all." Not too many Californians have forgotten their then-Governor's remark to conservationists wanting to preserve a few of the remaining original stands of the planet's most immense trees. When mature souls of Ronald Reagan's timbre are in charge, or in the majority, the loss of biodiversity can be swift and stunning.

At Earth's current juncture, if each small piece of life isn't guarded and treasured, if the lines to protect what you have aren't drawn firmly, you will continue to experience losses at a vastly increasing pace.

Do you keep your wetlands or allow them to be drained? Do you tolerate development when it kills endangered species? How many remaining wild areas do you accept being clear cut, dammed or made into golf courses? Is it all right for a paper company to pollute an area because then more people have jobs? Tradeoffs between risks and benefits must be considered, but decisions made now have strong impact. The time to protect biological diversity is instantly. Some planets become very barren. Either you plunge ahead, letting go of natural "entitlements", doing the right thing because you know its right (rather like falling in love with someone your heart picked though your mind would never) or you continue making compromises, coasting with status quo (though that sensible boyfriend is getting boring) while painting yourself into corners you may not escape from.

On Earth right now, many insects and seed types are lost daily; great numbers of larger animals are also lost each year. Diversity brings beauty to a planet, pleasure and excitement to its inhabitants—and security. Diversity is a safety net for all inhabitants. Sometimes those in charge will allow a planet to skid into austerity, losing up to 90-percent of its original life forms. Imagine how your Earth would look and feel at that point! A species which allows such a loss to occur carries ever after a certain sadness because life is never as rich and they know it. No planet can continue to support life in the customary way after such losses; only highly technological societies survive such devastation to their natural world.

NO MORE INFANTS, FEWER DEVAS

At some point during the mature soul period, all planets stop allowing new souls entry into the life stream. Also, new infant souls stop desiring to come because an already-mature world looks less appealing. Like Earth, most mature soul planets look and feel a bit worn. The wild devic places you all enjoyed in your earliest lifetimes are nearly gone. Would you choose Earth to start out on now?

Another reason new souls stop desiring to come is because playing catch-up to a majority three or four steps ahead is at best an uncomfortable strain. When so many are out in front, infant souls get pulled and stretched to move forward faster each lifetime and they can't so easily choose their own pace. Potential new souls also consider what scope they would have as young souls a thousand years hence. Would their creativity have much range or impact? Already the game is getting more refined and confined.

While this closure to new souls helps consciousness move along more quickly, nature, however, tends to have a more difficult time because there are fewer devas and nature spirits. Souls who are considering taking a series of lifetimes on a planet always check it out first in the form of nature spirits. If they are interested and curious about Earth, they can discover if they have an affinity with the planet and can leisurely decide if they wish to commit to a whole cycle of lifetimes on it. Back in the days, even a few hundred years ago, when Earth was loaded with nature spirits, people noticed them easily, and gave them names like sprites, fairies, elves and little people. They were rightfully seen to be protective spirits.

When in devic form, one has consciousness, intelligence, total oneness with nature and the Tao[4], but no physical body. To explore and know a planet, devic forms of life bind with different aspects of nature: these bonds help keep nature whole, strong and happy. When there are no longer large numbers of souls investigating a planet, nature is not as protected and consequently biological diversity is commonly lost. Some helpful overseeing

---

[4] Michael uses the term Tao, which means All-That-Is, undifferentiated oneness, to avoid confusion with the image of a bearded God in the sky.

devic activity will always remain, regardless, but never at earlier levels. This is always a part of the mature soul problem. How do you keep nature together without all that devic help? (However, just because devas aren't dancing around every tree doesn't mean you can't ask for their help with your garden, trees and part of nature—and get it.)

On Earth, just as on any planet at this juncture, there will be diminishing help from the unseen world at the very time all the due bills from the young soul era become glaringly apparent. The preservation and nurturing of life is now up to the sentient species inhabiting the planet. This is a major responsibility and a major fork in the road. If those in charge don't intuitively sense the need to protect, much diversity is inevitably lost. With "alarmist" types (like Al Gore) at the helm, a greater variety of life tends to be saved for future generations.

While the planet has many people rooting for sensible energy alternatives like solar and wind, others putting time, creativity and money into new, clean technologies and yet others committing to saving forests, threatened species, native seed stocks and so on, current trends do not yet favor nature. But, you do have a saving factor coming up, a shoe thrown in the works, some sabotage against man's progress by Mother Nature. Sabotage may not be a precise term, of course, but these natural reactions will help clean house and buy time.

ARISING VISIONS

When the world can't do business, or life, in the same old way, something new must be born; one advantage arising out of the trauma of the 90s will be the inability of countries and people to continue in the ecologically blind ways of the current period. The present system is self-destructive and obviously cannot last. Humans are being challenged to find a way of life which does not relentlessly take from the planet or steal from the children of the future. A sustainable economy, which neither poisons nor depletes resources, must be created. Politicians will no longer be able to appeal successfully to the lowest common denominator by arguing, for example, that cheap fossil fuels are a rightful part of your standard of living or that environmental and labor safety regulations must be relaxed because there is a recession.[5] It will soon be all too clear, probably even to Joe Sixpack, that economic and ecological health are inextricably linked.

Adverse environmental changes gradually push people into developing new ideas about how the world must look. By the year 1996, a pervasive and powerful vision is in place; large numbers of people sense what must be done. This vision is, of course, an ecological one: People know there is no future unless it is an ecological future. The critical mass necessary to make healthy choices in the U.S. will have finally collected itself. Europe comes to this point sooner; Australia a little later.

As humans begin to change their actions and ways of living, a beautiful sense of connection with the Earth takes root. In that mid-decade period, gratitude starts coming up when things go right—when food grows, when water flows, when the weather is benign. Currently, people tend to take these gifts from nature unconsciously and don't acknowledge the source of their abundance. A more reverent, appreciative, tuned-in state of mind will be forming.

With life not surging forward in the same materialistic, get-more-now kind of way, a pensive, even depressed interval will necessarily occur, followed by a determined and inspirational re-visioning stage. Many people will feel compelled to examine and modify their ideas about life, to look for meaning; no one wants their life to collapse into being solely about survival. As part of reinvesting in life and making existence seem worthwhile again, new images about life start arising and being discussed quite avidly, in day-to-day life and in the media.

A major world-wide reassessment will occur regarding

---

5 George Bush and John Sununu among others.

the environment, and about how jobs, industry, chemicals, technology, land use, agriculture, human and non-human life-forms—and cars—relate to the environment. This new vision necessarily involves respect for life's network of interconnections, and includes the understanding that whether you are pulling apart the fabric of life in a rain forest or in your own backyard, you are pulling apart needed human support systems. By the mid-90s, it is only too obvious that the ecological fabric must not be further picked apart. In fact, many people will be involving themselves in carefully weaving it back together.

ENVIRONMENT VS. MONEY

Rachel Carson's *Silent Spring* first stirred environmental consciousness in the early 60s. For the next three decades the spirit of materialism clearly beat out any spirit of deep change, but, as mentioned, the approaching mid-decade years will bring profound changes in point of view. Even highly educated Westerners will become more mindful of their linkage to natural systems. Many will feel a need to touch in with nature, to be in it, to hike in it and to take it into their hearts. As odd as this may sound, many people will be searching for a way to express their appreciation for and unity with forests, wild areas and wild creatures. This will be done with ritual—and increasingly with political action.

Those who live on the land, whether in Bali, Iowa, or dusty Timbuktu, have tended to be more mindful of their connections to natural systems than those who have lived in their heads, but now more and more humans will begin to see that saving endangered land, waterways or species will help save humans—also an endangered species.

What we see here is not so much a redirecting of society from above by the ecologically minded, but a grass-roots movement which shakes off the shackles of status quo and will no longer tolerate politicians or business leaders who lack the courage, conviction or common sense to make needed corrections. This movement may not even spout words like sustainable or regenerative, but revitalizing nature and creating a world with a better future will be the essence of what is naturally sought. As people become aware of the intense value of replanting forests and letting certain areas revert to wilderness, governmental dollars are likely to be channeled into these projects. The crucial importance of funding programs to heal the natural world finally becomes plain.

BIOREGIONALISM

While national support systems crack, shift and remain in flux, people will come to identify more strongly with their local communities. There will be some emphasis on buying local products simply because it works well on so many levels and helps the environment quite a bit. For instance, as an area starts to consciously depend more on local food production, regional diversity is supported because fewer monocrops will be grown for export to other areas; from pesticides to trucking, the load on the environment lessens dramatically.

Thinking local roots you in your area and makes you more committed to the health of your region. The now-tiny movement towards bioregionalism will grow. Mature souls enjoy having both a strong community identification and a strong global consciousness; when the two intertwine comfortably it feels like perfection. Urban or rural, you are happiest when you feel connected to your place, your own region of the world; when you appreciate the nearby people, cultures, woods, hills and land, the streams and lakes, the animals and even your area's unique blend of weeds and insects. Tuned-in like this, you know what needs protection or fixing and are more likely to be willing to fix it or fight for it. Politicians like to complain that no one wants anything (usually meaning something potentially dangerous, like an incinerator or halfway house) in their own backyard; but even when you are convinced that it's all one backyard, the only place most feel absolutely compelled to protect is usually close to home.

Living on marginal or too-crowded land where major amounts of food and raw materials must be imported is not an ideal circumstance at this time. Some countries, like Japan and the Netherlands, survive solely by virtue of imports. Both those countries create much of value for the rest of the world, but neither could exist at anywhere near current levels of abundance if the third world were to feed itself first. (Similarly, if rural areas in the third world were allowed to feed themselves first, most third world cities would quickly collapse.) In the U.S., as in Europe, the food situation is not currently critical because there is plenty, but as food production falls due to climatic strain, providing food to major cities will prove more difficult.

As we see it, if food could be distributed equitably there would be minimally enough for everyone right now only if Westerners would kindly drop their daily caloric intake to below 1500 vegetarian calories.[6] With people the way they are, that is unlikely to happen. But, with world population surging, feeding everybody at these minimums could last only a few years more, and does not factor in the increasing climatic changes and ecological problems which will make food production increasingly difficult. But that aside, within a few years of sharing those daily calories equitably among all people, your challenges would be greater than ever. Climate would be worse yet, soils, water and forests further depleted and the planet reeling from a still bigger crowd of hungry mouths.

The bloat and heart attacks of Europe and North America are based on food choices, but also on malnutrition elsewhere. There is going to be much debate, world-wide, as to whether poor countries should continue to export food (cash crops) or whether they should feed their own populations first. The mature

---

[6] Growing food on the hoof generally means there will be less food and water for humans to share. That, and the problem of cow methane adding very significantly to greenhouse problems, will make meat less appealing over time.

soul especially will be very concerned about morality here. Even an increasingly impoverished U.S. could afford to import high levels of food by making deals to knock down debt or interest payments for the countries involved, but is that fair? If these countries can't feed themselves, does it make sense to take bananas from them? Or for their prime agricultural land to be used for export sugar or cocoa instead of down-home beans? Or to collect interest payments from a country teetering on disaster, and then magnanimously give back a small percentage of that money as aid?

Europeans will be at the forefront, ending the practices they see as injurious. They may do so with boycotts or by placing high tariffs on tropical food imports to discourage their use. Wealthy third-worlders will struggle to hold their cash-crop system together for as long as they can, simply because it has made them rich. The multinational corporations controlling this trade will continue to exert strong behind-the-scenes pressure to maintain trade as it is. But the pragmatic and moral issues won't die away; they will be hotly discussed and impossible to sweep under the carpet.

The English may wonder about giving up their tea, but if the tea bush monopolizes valuable food growing land, it starts to seem the correct thing to do. The same with Americans and their coffee. At the very least, foods imported from countries not able to feed themselves will become more a luxury than now. Purchasing them may make you feel as incorrect as buying a fur may already. The sentiment in the developed world grows for third world countries to be given a fairer chance to make it.

Opinion will also be strong in first-world food-producing countries to keep food "at home" to help ensure supplies in chaotic times—even if that means people starve elsewhere. Since soothing consciences by sending shiploads of food will no longer be considered an option, public debate over what to do and what is fair will pick up considerably. Concern and guilt about mass sickness and starvation in the third world will enliven the search for answers to some bottom-line questions. Attention will go into analyzing systems and rooting out unjust practices. For example, the world will severely censure any government which is buying weapons and raising armies before attempting to feed itself.

With the emergence of mature soul consciousness, the excesses of the West become embarrassing and hard to stomach, especially as conditions in the third world become more pitiable. Western lifestyles will be seen to have been subsidized by the siphoning off of resources from the third world. Again, the older the soul, the greater responsibility one feels for correct action— and the greater sensitivity to the blind spots of your country. Thus, many mature and old souls will likely be among those most conscience-stricken about the increasingly awful state of poorer countries. Moral action will suddenly seem imperative.

The realization hits that U.S. deficit spending is part of the problem, and must be curbed; that third world debts need to be traded-off or forgiven in a way that protects everyone's future; that the practices of banks and multinationals need scrutiny and immediate modification; and that third world leaders must somehow be held accountable. This is not a short-term project, but it begins here because the world is ripe for change. Messages from the heart are no longer so easily neglected.

POPULATION

Because the first world has both the favorable land and fewer to feed, famine and pestilence will create more havoc in undeveloped, poorer, more powerless countries. The third world especially will see large increases in malaria, leprosy, tuberculosis, cholera, dysentery and AIDS. (If the weather does warm significantly in the early 2000s, diseases from the tropics will migrate into new territory, with Europe being particularly vulnerable.) With the strain on bodies from increased ultraviolet radiation, uneven food supplies, increased parasites and pervasive pollution, even once-simple flus can take deadly turns.

As increased ultraviolet radiation gnaws away at immune-system strength and integrity, diseases will more commonly jump species barriers, before now an unusual event. AIDS has already transferred from monkeys to humans. In another very unusual event, Soft Brain Disease in sheep became Mad Cow Disease as the ground remains of infected sheep were fed to cattle. Cats are now subject to their own brand of brain softening, transferred to them via beef pet food. The problems with farm factories raising animals with cost being the only bottom line will show up more clearly as human health deteriorates. When animals don't get sunlight, movement or healthy food themselves, their bodies don't exactly become healthy food for people to eat. Quality of life issues for the animals on these factory farms won't be ignored in a mature soul world.

What with food and disease problems and natural and ecological disasters, populations in Australia, Europe and the U.S. will likely decrease by 10 to 15-percent before the end of the decade; in Africa we expect about a 25-percent drop in population, but potentially up to 40-percent; China is likely to lose nearly 20-percent; India and Latin America 20 to 30-percent.

Does reducing worldwide population by 20-percent help ameliorate malnourishment in the world? In some places yes, but overall not greatly. For food to grow the weather must help, but even with bumper crops, politics must change or people still won't have food. Asia and Africa currently don't have enough food to go around. All possible tracts of land are being cultivated. Green revolution or not, there is not enough food.[7] If you cut the number of mouths to feed and the weather doesn't deteriorate, then more food becomes available per person—if, and this is a big if, it is fairly distributed instead of hoarded by the few or

---

[7] The green revolution of the 70s aimed to feed the world through scientific agriculture, but created myriad problems because of its heavy chemical emphasis and its discouragement of diversity.

exported to richer places.

South America has enough land to feed itself even at current population levels, but a good percentage of that land is tied up by landowners who won't allow it to go into food production. Rather, it lies fallow. This hard-edged, young soul tactic ensures a desperately needy labor force. When crop yields sag because of worsened growing conditions, fewer people in South America would not mean more food per person, unless more agricultural land was put into production.

CONTROLLING POPULATION 2000

With many people "shaken off", the Earth has an opportunity for some quiet healing. Souls on the astral plane will not be pressing so strongly to return. There will be no groups of newly arriving infant souls, and humans will be more conscious of their breeding habits. Though population plummeted initially because of planetary degradation, most countries realize the thing to do is to keep their numbers down and avoid the usual, unconscious, after-the-disaster occupation of breeding like crazy.

Population control becomes more talked about, more participatory and more creative in the new century, not more draconian. Birth control continues to improve and becomes increasingly easy to obtain and use. Abortion, also, will be more easily available. To the mature soul, it becomes inescapably obvious that unwanted pregnancies lead directly to child neglect, child abuse and a dozen other unacceptable social problems and that women who don't want to continue with a pregnancy ought not to be forced.

The emotional issues surrounding abortion will be carefully examined. Abortions always contain an element of sorrow because the soul trying to come in is usually an old friend, but it is not being allowed into (your) life, at least at that point in time. Calling abortion murder is not actually accurate because the soul is certainly not killed and, in fact, may even come right back to you in another pregnancy or as that little niece or god-child you so adore.[8] The soul of the child-to-be hovers around the pregnant mother, but does not enter its body until birth, and even then it is only lightly attached for the first two years. By early in the new century, abortion will be taken out of its current baby soul fundamentalist context and seen as an option, one that is nobody's first choice.

The methods by which population will be kept "low" will be myriad, with some systems clearly more kind than others. The biggest element is self-esteem, how women feel about themselves in the world. Happily for population figures, the way women are being viewed is under serious transformation at the moment. As the female sex's sense of power in the world rises, the need or desire for numerous children will drop drastically.

Both governmental programs and social pressure will combine to keep head-counts down. The content of public programs will stir debate in the coming decades. It will be seen that taking people who are destitute and enticing them into sterilization is just one more demeaning action that takes power away from the poor. How then do you get women to have one or two children, and not their culture's typical five or seven, when children (sons especially) are viewed as old age security? Getting to the root of the problem means giving poor women some sense of control over their lives. Sterilization will certainly still be encouraged with enticement tactics, but offering something more in return than a transistor radio or a half-month's wages to a person on the edge of starvation will seem vital. Rural water systems, sewers, schools, and clinics—these are the services that help make lives better and support people to decide on fewer offspring.

In fact, offering clean water, agricultural help, schools,

---

8 Murdering a person doesn't kill the soul either, of course, but it is a highly karmic situation because a soul becomes attached to a body through living in it. Also karmic is the fact
that other people have become attached to that person being in his body and are shocked and
pained when he suddenly and violently is not.

road repair, etc., to local communities as a reward for creating low fertility rates among themselves will be seen to be more conscious and workable than forced child quotas or sterilization. Local people immediately realize how their lives would be enhanced and enriched by these services. Let them figure out systems to cut birth rates—condoms or sterilization, rewards or penalties, education or whatever, and then give the promised help as birth rates actually fall. The community has then tripled its security: it will have a more supportable growth rate; the successful experience of pulling together to solve problems; and more security about health and jobs. Along with the memory of what it was like when the world was so crowded, these kinds of tactics can continue to hold down populations.

FIXES ON CONSUMPTION

Doing the right thing gets trickier when you think your purse or lifestyle may become threatened. Many people are so overwhelmed by the problems presented by conservation, including threatened price rises and job losses, that they fail to see the rewards that will accrue by backing away from polluting technologies and relentless consumption. Many new jobs in non-polluting technologies will be created. Before much longer, people discover that it doesn't take turning Texas on its ear to support solar research—or even to make a partial switch-over to solar.

Young souls go for expansion; mature souls appreciate the value of conservation. Conservation is usually pushed aside by politicians because even though you keep the world, it costs money now. The good news is that the communal will to adjust lifestyles and technologies so that the planet can continue to be home will be there by mid-decade. At that point, unless politicians are clearly on the side of cleanups and conservation of resources, they won't be very electable. Care with the environment becomes one more bottom-line people refuse to budge from.

Corporate leaders often fight conservation measures because to them regulations mean unwarranted government interference with their basic freedom to exploit resources. Business will rarely do the ecologically correct thing until it either gives them an edge on the competition or the competition is forced to do it too. When world environmental situations drastically change, politicians will find the courage, stamina and creativity to take on business and lead on environmental issues.

So how is it that this gets turned in a better direction? Suffering. People get less resistant to changing status quo when life isn't holding together anyhow. Suffering takes people to deeper, more thoughtful layers of themselves. The prior opulence of Western lifestyles starts to seem more distant and less appealing, or ethical; conservation starts to feel correct, not so bad. After all, you have already cut back! Furthermore, people are sufficiently scared by crop failures, pestilence, plant and human diseases that they become willing to take the cure, bite the bullet, and do exactly what is necessary to regain planetary health. Now you can get some leadership going on these issues.

Social pressure against non-essential consumption will be strong. There will be less product advertising to fan buying desires, and starting in 96 or 97 there will be blatant advertising propaganda which encourages ecological thinking and sustainable living. People will be sobered by little facts the media pitches at them, like, "Tiny Switzerland puts twice the burden on planetary resources as bulging-at-the-seams India."

The puzzle of how to manage the planet so that it won't collapse and can regain health and stability will grab many people's interest. How do you support life now and insure that your great-grandchildren can be supported too? This is the work of the next several decades.

THE NEW RELIGION

As the 90s move along, people in general will gain a certain reverence for nature. Tribal people often consider all life sacred and connected; peasants and farmers frequently feel a need to get in harmony with the natural world. However, once people became urban and sophisticated, connection with the environment tended to slip away. Now it starts to mend.

Humans, long disrespectful of nature and resources, can now sense that something is very wrong, so wrong that the chance of a big save by science is mighty slim. When people get so many curve and spit balls from nature they become fearful. Nature starts to become such an issue that, along with being more careful, people start doing more beseeching, whether it is prayer work, rainstorm dances, earthworks, medicine wheels, talking with nature spirits or asking for help from the goddess. This surge of feeling for the Earth has strong mystical and spiritual elements to it. Individually and collectively, a connection with nature suddenly seems vital. This new animism will help balance the weather; over time it will also help bridge the gaps between science and religion.

There is power in connecting and communicating with the environment, in moving back to basics, back to the Earth, and in being willing to go through the necessary detoxification process. People will know that as they connect with nature, they are connecting with a whole that is quite complex and beautiful. Nurturing nature will be done with wordless expressions of appreciation, with prayers and creative rituals, as well as with physical and political actions. This tuned-into-nature focus will be a theme picked up by many religions over the next thirty years, making a major turn from the Western mentality which took dominion over nature with the idea that God put it there for man to use. Manifest destiny, conquest of nature, exploiting resources, all that goes; those old concepts drain right out of politics, religion and the way most people think.

Religions will soon arouse and excite people's respect for the natural world, or they will start losing appeal. Greener churches will form to reflect changing consciousness. If a religion insists on no change, it's in trouble. Catholicism will probably capsize itself on this issue (and by sticking to its guns regarding the sin of birth control). Fewer and fewer will need rigid sets of rules about life. People are seeking love, communion with one another, with higher forces and with nature. They want ways of tuning into the living breathing Earth. They want to be part of its healing. This surge of Earth-centered activity and love does help create a healthier, more harmonious Earth.

The group of infinite souls, those Buddha and Jesus level beings, who will appear on the planet in the 2010 through 2020 era, will be speaking in luminous and powerful ways about the oneness of all life—plants, humans, cetaceans, animals, streams and mountains—and the importance of respect for the whole. These great beings will help people connect more deeply with each other and with nature. And you can be sure that they will be challenging the vested interests and rigid ideas they see around them, just like Buddha and Jesus before them.

THE ENVIRONMENT IN 2000

Right now the planet is dry, harsh, chemically afflicted, very uneasy, reeling from distress, and soon to get worse. By creating a ruckus, though, the Earth manages to clean itself, shake off some humans and decrease pollution. We believe that the natural world will probably start perking up late in the decade. Though ecological systems are still precarious, the Earth starts to feel more stable and happy. But there are still big questions. Will life support systems be able to cleanse and come into new balance? Will water and soil and air ever be able to sustain life as before? Will humans stick with the lessons of the 90s and behave ecologically or will they revert, taking whatever else they can?

By 98, agriculture will be practiced more sanely, meaning with fewer chemicals and more respect for the health of the soil. Herbicides and pesticides will be falling out of use because public outcry against them is so severe; they are seen as poisons, heavy-handed and not nearly clever enough. Clean food and vital soil are in. Safe, clever, biological controls against pests and weeds will be sought after. Scientists putting attention on food production will be coming at it from a more healthful, less arrogantly chemical standpoint than previously.

People will come to instinctually realize that supporting healthy life all over the planet means less trouble with the weather, pests, plant and tree diseases—as well as less human disease. Even a clever, non-toxic fix for corn blight or Dutch elm disease is different than actually creating healthy environments for plants to grow in. The morality and safety of genetic manipulation will continue to be debated, with the ethics and potential problems of these projects being carefully scrutinized.

CFCs will be banned before 1995. Fossil-fuel use will be heavily taxed—and falling. Safe, alternative energy sources will start receiving adequate development money. By the year 1997, people will have been so frightened by blights, epidemics and other breakdowns, that in hopes of turning adverse situations around, they become willing to do whatever is necessary to detoxify the planet. Clearly, this means getting chemicals out of the Earth's veins, getting rid of polluting practices, and living in a tuned-in fashion with new values to modify the current seriously materialistic ones. Humans will be discovering what non-material fulfillment means, looking to intimacy for it and to playful camaraderie, to spirituality, to adventure, and especially to community involvement and service. By 96 or 97, the majority is quite aware that the planetary crisis won't be solved by one more chemical or technological miracle and that the only way out will be hard questions, hard answers, some grace—and working creatively with decent politicians to get things done.

When bumped up against nature gone awry, mature souls will clearly see that humanity is part of nature; that nature is necessary to survival; and that they had personally better get a move on. Energetic local groups start to successfully counteract vested interests on local, and even on national and international levels. Citizens will be concerned enough about their communities to fight businesses, politicians and policies which do not conserve, make healthy or restore. The not-in-my-backyard syndrome, in which people gather together to fight degradation of their local area, is fierce by the year 2000, and is an important component in stopping the skid into deeper problems.

GAIA

The living, breathing planet does have consciousness of it-self and its parts, as well as the ability to adjust and regulate it-self. This consciousness is now popularly being referred to as Gaia, goddess of the Earth. On one hand, the Gaia energy is like Mother Nature, nurturing, giving, caring, non-judgmental, easily accepting whatever the kidlets are doing. It has provided abundance, beauty and grace for all to enjoy. Earth is a planet glowing with life. On the other hand, within the heart of the planet, its Gaia consciousness, there is growing frustration over the inability to maintain a balanced, smoothly functioning planet; too many people and too many polluting practices continually intensify the strain. With holes in every ecosystem, and much of life going awry, it is not surprising to find uneasiness and agitation within the planet itself, within Gaia.

This human experiment could simply be allowed to go where it goes, even if it shoved the Earth towards freezing, arid conditions like Mars, cloudy and boiling conditions like Venus, or become too poisoned and toxic for life, like more than a few previously pleasant planets. But those scenarios do not seem to be what is preferred, or likely. The Gaian urge, as far as we can see, is to keep the planet relatively stable by keeping temperatures consistent, water flowing, air fresh, gases mixed normally and photosynthesis hopping so that all aspects of life may continue to thrive.

The Gaia energy is far more personal than the totally neutral energy of the Tao or God. We see it as a large coalition of devic beings, a collection of souls who chose eons ago not to be physical at all, but to be the keepers of nature and protectors of the Earth. This group or coalition became essentially the energetic overseers of the planet, and its soul. It appears to us as a million points of light that hover close, all around the planet on a triangular sort of grid, and as light radiating from the core of the planet to each of those points of light. The grid has give and flux, even as it helps keep the Earth stable. At this moment, however, the grid is losing some cohesiveness; it is shabby, not in great shape. Patches of it have come loose, like shingles on the top of a house being rumpled or blown off.

Letting the planet's more primal energy loose will essentially be a reassertion of Gaian power. It is the power of the planet unleashed to effect its own healing. Through this organic, chaotic process a smoother functioning whole than presently exists will be created.

Like a tossed pebble rippling the water around it, what one person does makes a difference. As the planet becomes more chaotic, appearing sometimes even to come apart at the seams, each person who can remain stable and centered makes a difference in the way life feels for all. As you ground and heal yourselves and get rid of your personal chaos, your new level of wellbeing, and your example, helps others heal their fear of change. Also, you may now find yourself a person with something important to say and to offer, a leader.

EXERCISE

The following is a simple, very profound consciousness exercise designed to plunge you into deep layers of yourself.

Pair up with a friend to do this. Sit across from each other and look into each other's eyes. Maintain a gentle eye contact throughout. The younger person will ask the older a question from the list below and then quietly, openly listen as the person responds. Time this for five minutes. The questioner is to give no feedback at all, simply be present and still. If the respondent stops talking, gently repeat the question.

When five minutes is up, quietly switch roles, with the older person asking the younger the same question. As before, the questioner stays quiet and aware, but non-responsive.

When that is complete, do another round with the same question. This will seem ridiculous and hard to do, but do it to get the experience.

If you are feeling adventuresome, you may wish to do another round after that, or a round using one of the alternate questions.

THE QUESTIONS
Where does happiness come from?
What is contentment?
What is Gaia?
What is Earth?

CHAPTER 5

The World Report
Political Changes/Earth Changes

Men and nations behave wisely once they have exhausted
all the other alternatives.
—*Abba Eban*

Too bad the only people who know how to run the
country are busy driving cabs and cutting hair.
—*George Burns*

SOUL AGE PROGNOSIS

One valuable aspect of the concept of soul age lies in being able to analyze the potential scenarios in any individual country based on who is in it, what their capabilities and limitations might be. Incorporating a soul-age diagnosis with some understanding of the given social and political conditions in a particular area leads to clearer perceptions of how a country might adjust and refashion itself under increasing economic stress and the onslaught of ideas now coming into focus.

You'll find that in any country it makes a huge difference

not only what the largest soul-age group is, but also what group is second largest. For instance, Haiti is primarily baby but contains nearly as many infant souls, making it less likely to move forward and develop than India and China, also primarily baby but with their next strongest input coming from surging young soul populations.

Checking to see what's in the wind, we'll scan the world, first taking a look at infant soul areas, then at the whole globe, continent by continent, specifically examining many individual countries. We'll pay special attention to the up-and-coming batch of young soul countries, which are always interesting and always potentially troublesome.

INFANT SOUL COUNTRIES

Countries with large infant soul populations are quite naturally undeveloped, affording those souls who are beginning their human experience the slower, simpler lifetimes they desire. Infant souls often find themselves in skirmishes with nature and climate, marginal food situations, marauding tribes and warring neighbors. Enduring these types of hardships are part and parcel of learning about survival on earth.

It is exceedingly difficult to economically develop a nation composed primarily of infant souls because the population simply doesn't have the backlog of experience or skills on which to build. This inexperience can make a big difference in even such a seemingly modest arena as producing crafts for possible sale to the many tourists now exploring these (See it before it's gone!) primitive areas. Infant souls rarely come up with the ideas, discipline, craftsmanship, or the sales pizzazz to take advantage of this potential influx of cash.

When an infant soul area is doing well, as it has for thousands of years in the heretofore well-protected Amazon Basin, those early lifetimes can feel very aligned with nature, rich and special. Now, many indigenous Amazon tribes are losing their traditional lands, and with it their buffer zones of protection from the outside world—as well as from each other. Losing territory also means your food supply shrinks. Amazonian tribes will continue losing ground throughout the 90s, though at declining rates because the area has found many, many protectors in the form of ecologists, journalists, rock stars, and even the occasional politician. Tribal peoples, currently about 40% infant and 35% baby, are seeing increasing numbers of young, mature and old souls born among them, people who desired front row seats—or starring parts—in the fight to save these cultures, their knowledge, and the rain forest itself.

Tribal lives in Borneo, New Guinea and Australia will remain fairly stable throughout the 90s, being neither terribly plagued by development nor wracked by climatic changes. Ethiopia, the Sudan and Somalia are in dire shape with little chance for improvement over the next twenty years. This area is severely overpopulated, ecologically devastated, warring with itself and unlikely to change for the better. Sri Lanka has descended into warring with itself too, with its population changing from the baby/young ferment of twenty years ago to the baby/infant combination of today. Being unwilling or unable to pull itself out of the fighting pushes this country, or any country, more deeply into impoverishment on almost every level. Sri Lanka could be an island of delight—but so could every place.

Infant souls understandably don't have the confidence or knack for changing much about their world, especially when it is going awry. Nor do they have the power to stand up to young souls, the landlords, warlords, shopkeepers or government officials most likely to be making their lives more wrenchingly difficult (as in rural Central America where lives are threatened, made miserable and tenuous by political corruption and greed). Infant souls have little interest in or comprehension for politics, but it is politics which nevertheless often makes their lives insecure and wretched.

Ambitious young souls doing their thing in equatorial areas are the folks most likely to be bumping up against the infant soul and causing trouble. Young souls are pushing into the Amazon to farm, ranch and mine; they are sparring for power in Central America; vying for control of Peru and Columbia; and playing politics with food in Ethiopia, Somalia and the Sudan. Remember, everybody who is now mature or old has had his lifetimes of terrorizing the peasants, the serfs, the peons, the natives, the slaves, the factory workers—and the women. Karmic, you bet, but it simply goes with young soul turf. Where young souls gather, this behavior will continue, though under closer scrutiny than ever before, and with many more restraints on it.

LATIN AMERICA

South America and Central America (as well as most of the Caribbean countries) are predominately poor baby soul countries run by the usual gang of rich young souls, well-born and clever enough to maintain the social policies which have kept the money in their family pockets for generations. Status quo is usually easy to maintain, for the baby soul masses are more comfortable with tradition, even when it pinches them badly, than with change. Change seems risky, dangerously tipping the boat when not completely sure of your ability to swim.

Typically, baby souls will think exactly along the lines they've been taught and do what their leaders say to do, for what they are working on, internally, is learning to obey a given society's unique set of rules. Old rules which seem to carry the weight of tradition feel better than any newfangled way of looking at life: if the religion says do this, and has been saying that same thing for centuries, then it must be right. This soul age can get internally panicked just listening to someone railing against a landlord, much less proposing political change, because that might mean recasting the traditional order.

Because baby souls are the largest group in Latin America,

politicians, the clergy, business and landowners have had a relatively easy time sucking profit from their complacent, low-paid labor pool, without giving much back in the way of salaries or services. Though their churches may be ornate, these people usually don't get paved roads, sewers, electricity, healthcare, education, or enough regular work to purchase adequate food. Nevertheless, baby souls are likely to remain loyal to their leaders, often thinking of them as superior people, strong fathers who had best be obeyed. Igniting a revolution with this kind of majority is like using damp kindling to start a fire. In baby soul countries, established leaders tend to be admired wholeheartedly, unless they attempt to fast-forward the masses. (This being the main reason the Shah of Iran was booted out as he attempted to foist a modern, westernized life on the country's increasingly baby and infant population. It wasn't so much the Shah's extravagance, corruption or police tactics, for all of those traits can be ignored by the baby soul, but his strong push for modernization that brought down the reign.)

Until now, these soul-age patterns in Latin America have been fairly stable since colonial times. What is currently happening in about half these countries is a shock to tradition; an increasing number of young souls are being born into families which have been poverty-stricken for generations. Many, now in their teens and twenties, can neither imitate nor abide the stoicism of their parents. Young souls are all here-and-now. Praying for a better afterlife does not make sense to them; this is the life that must be worth something. They have experienced heartless landowners, seen siblings or cousins die from lack of medicine and parents weak and sick from grueling work. They know what it is to have too little food and fuel and water. Now, that gangbuster young soul energy of theirs is pushing them to get out there and make something happen. But, what's to do? How can they possibly shape life to their liking?

Finding few decent work opportunities in rural areas and

no place for their individualism or ambition to go, they are migrating in hordes to large cities where few jobs await them; even
an informal street business selling fruit or handicrafts requires
some capital, savings they don't have. Banks rarely lend to the illiterate poor. Soon it's discovered that the police often bleed
street businesses dry, anyhow. The cards are stacked against them
no matter which way they turn. These *desperados* don't expect
job training or other educational opportunities, but when they
discover no jobs and dismal business prospects, the only door
open may be petty crime.

These up-and-coming young souls can't be controlled; if
continually frustrated, they can get mean. Increasingly, they are
making life miserable for the rich all over Latin America, most
particularly in Brazil, but also in Argentina, Peru, and in an orga-
nized-crime fashion, in Columbia. Life in cities like Rio is an
increasing headache for anyone with money. You can't wear jew-
elry or carry a bag or package. Nothing is safe, not even your
person. It used to be tall stone walls with glass shards atop them
would keep the poor out, but now around-the-clock guards at
your walls may not be enough. Everything gets stolen. Car
alarms protected cars until thieves figured how to get around
their noise, in seconds. So, the rich bought systems which closed
down gas lines within a few miles should their vehicle be hot-
wired. Subsequently, more cars were stolen with their owners in
them, at knife or gunpoint, some crooks taking delight in leaving
car owners naked on isolated roads—not at all a (prudish) baby
soul behavior.

So many fractious characters being born into lower classes
means times have changed; the masses can't be so easily controlled. The police actually kill street kids as one way of holding down crime. Now, these children of the streets are protest-
ing, marching by the thousands, grabbing headlines. It is a revolution starting to happen, a punch from below which will force
rich Latin families to create openings and opportunities for at

least some of the poor. If these wretched masses don't get a healthy way to participate in society, the crime wave will turn uglier yet.

The ruling families are nervous, but not changing their ways—except for taking more pains with security. In an attempt to protect themselves in case everything blows, many transfer money outside their country and continent instead of investing at home. This drains cash from local economies, tending to make everybody poorer and the situation as a whole more tense. Argentina, Brazil, Columbia, Peru, Venezuela, Central America and Mexico greatly need to make social, political, land, educational and economic adjustments to avoid descent into internal chaos.

Clearly there is transformation going on already in Latin America. Military dictatorships are falling away, one by one. Two countries, Brazil and Chile, have popularly elected presidents for the first time in twenty years and it looks as if democracy is holding, inside and out. The fellows with uniforms and guns are minding their manners; the U.S. and its CIA are also minding their manners, not interfering as they did twenty years ago when both Brazil and Chile's democratically elected leaders were murdered. With the U.S. and the Soviets no longer fighting wars of influence in Latin America, Latin politics will be left alone to a much greater extent, allowing for more freedom, more creativity and better self-regulation.

The birth control question in Catholic Latin America is still too mined to tackle effectively, but because cities are at such bursting points, it is finally clear that doing whatever it takes to support rural people to remain in rural areas is a good deal for everyone. People need services in the countryside, services that always go to cities, capitals first, to keep city dwellers placated and away from presidential palaces. But, to be viable, rural areas need the support of schools too, and electricity, sewers, health services and so on. Latin governments won't find the money to add extensive improvements overnight, but many are finally seeing rural services as useful and important. Times have changed.

Currently, the U.S. is pushing hardest at Columbia and Peru, but Bolivia and Ecuador are being pushed too, to destroy drug-producing crops and labs. With a peasantry barely able to eke out a living cultivating easy-to-grow, high-payoff (illegal) crops, how possible is it to switch? How can you bomb their land with herbicides and defoliants if you are then destroying their ability to survive? To effectively lower drug production you must not only come up with alternate crops but make sure these people will be able to extract a living from the substitutes. This kind of thinking is social progress. These countries are now more interested in making rural reforms than they are in heavy-handed requests from the U.S. to spray the land with poisons and put the peasant growers out of commission. This too is change.

Most Colombians, including many politicians, now want to get rid of the dark shadow cast by drugs, drug deals and drug money. Colombia is sophisticated and rich enough that it is capable of transforming itself from a drug money capital to something more diversified and positive. To pull this off, both determination and vision are needed. Colombia has enough solid young souls, creative mature souls, infrastructure, and new-found vision and purpose that it is unlikely to descend into chaos.

Peru may. It is not in good shape and its center is not holding. It is poorer, its people not so widely educated. High debt, lack of food, fewer mature and young souls, plus the Shining Path guerrillas who want to pull the country apart, will probably work together to pull the country apart. Life will grow more punishing yet.

Venezuela is a richer country. It has a large (nearly 25%), stabilizing group of young souls determined to hold on to their money and country. They intend to manage the poor and the military in whatever way necessary to insure their future.

However, with nearly half its citizens so poor they can only afford one meal a day, economic reforms are clearly required to avoid further problems with uprisings. Venezuela will keep itself stable, either by making sufficient reforms or by becoming increasingly authoritarian and brutal.

Latin countries which are not already being pushed politically and socially by segments of their poor are likely to remain fairly stable during the coming economic crunch. Most of them have large proportions of baby and infant souls, who tend to remain quiet and conservative, even when burdened by increasingly extreme poverty. Potentially, these countries could be inflamed by some brand of political righteousness, but that appears unlikely. Baby souls have a desire to fit in and live closely within the confines dictated by their society. They need to feel right about what they are doing—in Latin America (and Africa) this usually keeps them quiet. (In Arab countries it is getting them noisy.)

In most Latin countries, mature souls account for, at minimum, 20% of the population. Mexico is unique in that it has had a strong mature soul influence for many centuries, through most of its cultures and transformations. Over the last hundred years it has had essentially equal numbers of mature and baby souls. Being a country with such a vital mature soul influence gave Mexico its vibrant art and creativity, also its warmth of family and community connections. While mature souls are usually able to boost a country's economy, they were not able to give Mexico much of a lift because of the low priority this non-intellectual society puts on education.

The border between the U.S. and Mexico is the only first world/third world border on the globe. That it has been peaceful is partially because it leaks so well and partially because of traditional Mexican docility. When times get rougher and severe food shortages arise in both countries, the border will become a sore spot as the U.S. more willfully tries to close it in order to feed and care for its own population first.

AN ASIDE

Now, while it is true that the 15% who are wealthy in Latin America (or anywhere) have tended to be young souls grabbing easy birthrights on their way to experiences of power and wealth, there are always exceptions. Any soul age can take well-heeled births, but because money and power are such a quintessential young soul experience, these wealthy births tend to be more wearing for the other soul ages. Hard to believe? Imagine yourself the daughter of Donald Trump, or a son who is expected to continue with a family business, where high profit is based fairly directly on the misery of its workers. Being born into situations like these is a piece of cake for the young soul, but compromises both the morality and freedom the later soul ages hold dear, and often forces a difficult rebellion.[1]

Young souls, of course, choose to be born poor also—sometimes just to get going with a body, there being too few rich parents to go around. But also they do it in order to challenge themselves and gain strength through willfully rising above miserable circumstances, similarly to how a baby soul might choose to test her mettle by incarnating into a rich, competitive family in order to be pushed toward greater responsibility.[2] An individual will always find something interesting in going against the grain.

Old souls tend to choose their birth locations carefully so as to have some degree of comfort and stability. Nevertheless, they generally make up at least one-percent of primitive populations too, where they take on care-taking positions like teacher, shaman, storyteller, herbalist, midwife or healer for the community. Sometimes old souls also choose powerful, wealthy parents in order to put themselves in a position to get things done for the

---

[1] John Robbins is a good example of this, plunging forward to improve the diet of America as he rejected the "karma" of the Baskin-Robbins ice cream fortune. He is the author of *Diet for a New America*.

[2] Queen Elizabeth is an example here.

world. Of course, the danger lies in getting too lazy or too compromised to challenge the family conscience or come fully into their own depth and truth.

Mature souls exist in every culture too, at about five percent minimum. They incarnate wherever they can learn, express and create with emotion—which is basically worldwide. Some mature soul gathering spots, like Hollywood, Rio, Amsterdam or Rome are much more pleasant than others, say Prague or Rangoon, but growth through emotional intensity is universally available, so mature souls aren't usually as picky about their birth locales as the old soul becomes. Of course, what has tired the old soul and made her prudent and selective is the intense experience of those very mature soul lifetimes.

AFRICA

From most every angle, Sub-Saharan Africa looks to be a sad, increasingly difficult place to live with continued adverse climatic changes, worsening drought, pestilence and famine, rampant AIDS and malaria, plus the usual tyrannies inflicted by leaders interested primarily in their own personal aggrandizement. The first world (with its hands still in Africa's pockets) will increasingly turn its back on Africa, with the Somali Operation Restore Hope intervention likely to prove an anomaly. Over the next two decades, Africa is likely to find few success stories and little rebirth.

It is for several reasons that the world will increasingly let this continent falter and drift. First, the developed world is having a difficult time itself and is thus pulling attention homeward. Second, it is increasingly possible to ignore Africa because wars between the Soviets and the West are no longer being waged here. Without foreign military help and money, no African country is big or sophisticated enough to be a major threat on the world scene. Third, Africa appears depressing to the Western eye. AIDS has spread like wildfire. Nothing seems

to work or change for the better; life continues to fall back on itself. Problems don't have easy solutions and corruption abounds.
Africa appears to be a sinkhole to Western governments, which
are increasingly unwilling to throw money into it despite mam-
moth suffering. Development money and business loans are
heading toward Eastern Europe, which needs to be brought forward by 20 years, not 200. Africa has been set adrift, left to its
own internal chaos and pain. The (unspoken) first world feeling
is, Let it sink; perhaps it will cleanse itself in the process.

In general, it is fair to say that Africa's leaders have not
been stewards who helped their countries along (though the few
who did were hassled by the West). Rather, they have tended to
be a corrupt, fanatical and maladroit bunch. At best, they have
tended to skim money off for personal use, institute a few
grandiose projects, and ignore basic health and educational services for their citizens. (Overall, though, their money-grabbing
looks puny compared to the ways first world policies have
squeezed the continent.) But despite bad leaders and poor treatment from the rest of the world, Africa's most horrendous problems are now coming from a disastrously worsening climate and
booming populations which have come close to exhausting the
land.

Some places, like Mozambique, had excellent leaders and
could have developed beautifully but for the policies of the West
and South Africa, which were bent on keeping any potentially
strong socialized (or black) country down. Mozambique received incredible pain and injury in the "destabilization" process,
but might still recover if South Africa's disruptive policies towards it were halted and the West would pitch in with (guilt?)
money. This country, though, must also handle its ethnic disharmony and intertribal warfare in order to move forward.

South Africa, for so long controlled by legions of thick,
white baby souls, is finally trying to create breathing room for
all races. Will it manage? Many here are doing their honorable

and stubborn best to make the changes that will hopefully insure that their world does not descend into gross chaos. Nevertheless, fear, anger, and stinky, corrupt politics abound, among both whites and blacks. The country has wealth, resources and much of the determination it needs to move carefully forward and avoid the all-too-easy slip into total, bloody mayhem.

Over half the country's remaining whites are at least acquiescent to change, convinced by economic sanctions that their world must somehow be slowly and carefully opened to blacks. It is a scary process requiring courage and a great deal of moral strength. Among the whites there is a 20% strong, almost totally baby soul contingent of people, who would rather see the country in war and ruins than co-ruled by blacks. They exude a frightened, stubborn, vigilante mentality and are angry, in that inimical baby soul way, over the traditional order shifting so radically beneath their feet. Another 30% can't decide which is worse, a possible bloodbath and continued world sanctions against South Africa or opening up their world to blacks. They waver back and forth, tortured inside.

The blacks have been so suppressed, repressed and shoved into corners that those who are politically active tend to be very angry. The whites got their reeducation from the world at large in the last few years. The blacks now need some reeducation in order not to get mired in righteous anger, resentment and impatience. They need help in pulling themselves out of futility and in getting creative with the new possibilities starting to appear. The black townships could greatly benefit from traveling consciousness teachers, whether Werner Erhard's est teachings or Maharishi's Transcendental Meditation or any kind of motivational teachings preaching self-responsibility, forgiveness and moving forward. Because so many blacks are mature souls, they can be reached relatively easily with this type of support. They are living historical, transitional lifetimes as the world opens up this way; it would help to have a sense of themselves in history and to gain perspective on how transitions are normally two steps forward and one back. They need overviews, and they need the understanding that their self-esteem will gradually heal itself. With realism and psycho-spiritual support, this community would be better prepared to move forward as opportunities open.

Potentially, South Africa could become slightly glorious; it has the ingredients. This best-case scenario, which would need to be founded on slow, steady rebuilding and education, has about a ten-percent likelihood right now. The worst-case scenario, a big bloody mess with the economic infrastructure ruined, still has about a 25% probability.

After dry conditions in the early years of the decade, the weather in South Africa appears to be fairly benign. The country will be shaken by several earthquakes with a Richter force of 7.0 or higher during the decade of the 90s, and will be forced to cope with problems caused by the severe lack of ozone protection in these southern regions.

It is an extremely difficult situation, but at least South Africa's white leaders have been called on their tyranny and forced by world opinion and economic sanctions to consider changing to join the late 20th century world. Africa's black leaders, many of whom are even more tyrannous toward their own race, have not yet been pushed to their knees by world pressure, though the governments of Kenya and Zaire are starting to feel the glare of the world spotlight. The West and Saudi Arabia both have a strong commitment to keeping Kenya stable, so it is being spurred to become responsive to all classes and tribes of people, democratic in other words. Though it is primarily baby souls (35%), its nearly as large proportion of young souls (30%) gave Kenya the ability to forge ahead of other African countries.

The whole inner core of Africa is most affected by AIDS, which will continue spreading and decimating poor populations. Too little food, not enough protein and high rates of venereal diseases do not bode well for immune-system strength, making the march of AIDS and related problems easy and swift. The pain in these central areas is already intense and is due to worsen considerably.

West Africa has several countries which are heading towards young soul expressions: Ghana, the Ivory Coast, and Liberia. Each of these countries will be trying to knock down the one-sided trade policies which have drained resources and raw materials from them without giving much back in the way of wealth or jobs. These countries might start fighting back, for instance by sitting on their raw materials and produce (and debt repayments if they dare) until Western trade policies are changed. Western Africa looks fortunate in that it is likely to retain a climate that supports steady food production.

Nigeria, also heading towards young, will likely become increasingly militaristic, authoritarian and difficult for its neighbors. Cameroon looks as if it will be ripped apart by its own military forces.

THE MIDDLE EAST & NORTH AFRICA

With both fundamentalism and political leaders fomenting self-righteous tendencies, the baby souls in this area are not so quiet. Khomeini, who is still revered as a saint by most of his countrymen, made Iranians feel extraordinarily noble and pure at heart in their battles with devil America and wayward Iraq. Saddam Hussein, to the amazement of the Western world, reached again into that baby soul need for ironclad righteousness (and pied-piper leaders), even when his path seemed to go against all logic, self-interest and self-preservation. But, especially to baby souls, losing lives and property may seem worth it when the cause promises to ennoble you.

The level of uneasiness a baby soul experiences with foreign ways of life, or even slightly varying sects, cuts deep into the mentality of this group because of their need to live by unyielding, infallible sets of rules. Even though economic reconstruction takes focus and energy, both Iran and Iraq are likely to remain tinderboxes of emotion—and thorns in the side of more moderate Arab leaders who fear their citizens being pricked by the same fundamentalist fervor.

Iran is disillusioned, sobering up and rebuilding, its people suffering the economic devastation caused by pulling away from the rest of the world. It did not win its war with Iraq; "Devil America" is doing fine and the Soviets have cut off funds. On top of that, 1990's catastrophic earthquake was such a crushing blow that the general populace suddenly had the feeling it had gone wrong somehow. People were pushed inward, and in Iran much internalized contemplation is still going on: God causes earthquakes, but why not to America or Iraq? Why here?

Anywhere they strike earthquakes always shake up self-satisfaction and that which is rigid, including thinking. Iranians are now more thoughtful, more reflective and the country is calming down, becoming mindful again of the rules of civilized behavior. Being an island unto themselves was not as satisfying an experience as expected. Nevertheless, power issues still abound.

Rafsanjani, Iran's present leader, an early young soul and a much more practical person than Khomeini, is an effective manager of the country's economy. With the help of the U.S., China, North Korea, Russia, Argentina, Germany, Italy and France, he has built his military into a hunky, sophisticated machine. It will not go unused. (Before too very long, mature soul ethics will make these lucrative, already shady weapons deals much more difficult and offensive.) Iran may try expanding into one or more of the newly unleashed, primarily Moslem republics of the former Soviet Union. And it may bully the whole area with dark threats of devastation.

The Gulf war, which consisted of bombing the hell out of Iraq, did exactly that to a degree because it siphoned off some craziness and delusions of grandeur. The war served as a reality check; most people are back to their everyday lives, sobered. On the other hand, the bombing left huge reservoirs of humiliation and pain which await the next leader with promises of victory. Everything has repercussions: war, bullying and covert activity, as well as diplomacy and a positive sense of possibilities.

Iraq is still posturing. Though people feel worn and defeated, they could take their minds from suffering and be rallied again in a bid to save face. Overall though, visions of military glory are fading, being replaced by desires for food and stability. But still, there may be flare-ups for a considerable while. Wounded pride doesn't disappear quickly, especially in this area of the globe, and the boundless stubbornness of leaders never helps.

Khomeini was a baby soul whose vision centered on purity and righteousness, while young soul Saddam Hussein's vision is of personal power expansion. Though Iran now has young leadership, it is a baby soul country with a fairly large proportion of infant souls still being born. Iraq is baby also, but with strong young and mature soul elements—which are getting wiped out in the post war slide of the middle class into poverty.

Saudi Arabia, Kuwait and the other oil-rich Gulf States are all young soul hangouts which have heavy (baby soul) religious influences. Underlying each of these countries is a powerful, rigidly practiced form of Islam which pervades every aspect of life. For example, opening Saudi Arabia to even a highly censored form of television required a major diplomatic effort with the keepers-of-Islam who are suspicious of anything not approved in the Koran (625 A.D.). The ruling Kings and Princes tend to be young and mature souls and must contend with the mullahs, who tend to be baby and young, and conservative. The royal rulers have reality-based fears of disturbing even one hair on the head of the mullahs, making it extremely difficult to change any aspect of social or cultural life in these societies.

When men from the Gulf States travel, they break almost all the rules, including allowing their wives to be seen in Parisian street clothes, but for now it feels correct and comfortable enough to come home to the orthodoxy they were raised with. The occasional woman is impatient to make changes, but would risk her life to agitate directly, and, at any rate, has little power to affect outcomes in these most male of societies. Not too far in the future these stringent restrictions on female life will loosen, though marginally. In the meantime, any movement towards increased social freedom must be made cautiously, with fear of grave consequences. First oil and business, then the affordability and seduction of Western goods, and recently the soldiers of the Gulf war served to dislodge these Arabian countries, a quarter inch at a time, from their rigid ways and fears of foreign influences.

The Saudi rulers view themselves as the rich patriarchs and caretakers of the Moslem world. This they take quite seriously, though their poorer cousins in the other Arab nations don't think they do enough and are nearly always more resentful than thankful. The Saudi family's young soul practicality and easy grasp of world and corporate politics stabilized the country early on, even preparing it for potential declines in oil consumption. (By about 1997, oil usage will have fallen significantly due to economic difficulties, the thinning out of human populations and new technologies pushed into existence to cut down on carbon dioxide emissions.) Even with a lowered demand for oil and falling returns on investments, the Saudi's will remain powerful, rich and secure, unless a worst-case scenario plays itself out in the area—but more on that in a moment.

Kuwait is composed of nearly fifty-percent young souls, most of whom grew too arrogantly lazy to work—even to scramble to put their post war country back in business. A quiet kind of decadence set in here in this small country, a softness which was like a perfumed calling card to Saddam Hussein—he knew they were too much into palatial plush to be in fighting shape.

Since it usually comes with the turf, why aren't all these

young soul Kuwaitis more alert and aggressive and on top of their world? Life was so easy it baked initiative and purpose right out of them, often competence too; luxuriating in easy money and self-satisfaction, they didn't bother to develop themselves or their talents. Challenging lifetimes get you going; easy and sumptuous have major downsides, for countries as well as for in-dividuals. Kuwait will be shaky for a long while. Aside from money, they have few resources with which to heal or rebuild. Kuwaitis will continue to feel like displaced rich people, not at home or really secure anywhere, including in their own country.

Syria and Israel, the other young soul countries in the re-gion, are military powerhouses. Prior to the 70s, Syria was a mature soul enclave, secular, even slightly racy and liberal. Mid-young since then and under Hafez Assad's unrelenting, iron-fisted (young soul) rule, it is likely to fall back further in soul age dur-ing the 90s. Its gates of opportunity are not open wide enough for young soul tastes. Assad could have had a much stronger and more powerful country if he had chosen to develop the abilities of this population instead of suppression and slaughter.

Israel's development as a heavy-duty military power helped mend the World War II shredded psyches of its citizens by proving it could beat its Arab neighbors back onto their heels, again and again, a most satisfying young soul experience. Instead of ever making accommodations, showing compassion or respect, Israel relied on its own brand of baiting, bullying and swagger (and its American-financed military capacity). No doubt this behavior meant survival then; now these same behaviors are not survival oriented. Although Israel is edging towards a mature soul expression, it is kicking and screaming all the way. The huge influx of Russian Jews will help to push it further along the soul-age scale so that soon it will find some intention of getting along with its neighbors, rather than simply flexing muscle to keep them intimidated. Sounds unbelievable, right?

From a young soul mind-set you think it is fair to use all

the power you can muster to try to control all of life, but from a mature soul place you know there are things you should not do. Israel is at this very juncture, clinging tenaciously to the power patterns that have worked in the past. It is a scary transition for a person or a country to make. If you let go and move forward, which a part of you is inclined to do, it looks as if you will lose control and be defenseless, unable to avoid bad situations. Any of you who have ever had to stop trying to control a relationship and let it take its own course understand what this stage feel like: a glimmer of freedom twinkles at you to take courage, wade through your fears and let go, while conservative parts of you scream: No, don't let go. Insist on what you want on your own terms.

In the Arab world, Israel is a focal point for anger against the more powerful West. It is also an excuse for Arab failure, an easy scapegoat. At any rate, with Israel moving ever so slowly towards a more embracing perceptivity, and world pressure now on both Israel and Syria to mind their military manners, the equation in the Middle East will change for the better. Seething resentments towards Israel from its Arab neighbors won't go away, but the timing is right for some common sense cooperation among all parties. If Clinton continues to pull the U.S. back from its automatic knee-jerk support of Israel, Arabs will at last feel as if their side is being heard—instead of being rudely run over. They are angry to their cores about being treated as no-counts at the creation of Israel, and often since. This change in stance by the West is essential to begin the healing in the Middle East.

Once again, with Moscow and Washington no longer fighting each other for an edge here, something better can evolve. The (mature soul) world attitude coming into play insists that it is time for all the parties to sit down with each other to talk, shatter old rigidities, hatreds and opinions, and somehow come to compromise, understanding and peace. These ideas were promoted by both Bush and Gorbachev, who formerly had been egging on Middle Eastern hostilities.

Libya and Yemen are primarily baby and infant. Libya also has a fair-sized technological-minded young soul cast, while Yemen has a good contingent of mature souls, who join everybody else to relax and chew qat, a mild narcotic, every afternoon. Yemen now has so few young souls that much of the land previously devoted to cultivating their famous mocha coffee has now been dug up to grow qat, which interestingly not only brings no money into the country but cuts into everybody's productivity. (Humans love creating endless varieties of experience for themselves.)

Lebanon was a comfortable mature soul country not so many years ago, full of cafés, beauty and vacationing Europeans. Now it is a torn-up wreck. Its young souls aren't productive, but wild with warfare: there is no escape from intense, wrenching experience here. Like Yugoslavia for Eastern Europe, Lebanon serves as a warning for all Arab countries, exemplifying what happens to a country when citizens stubbornly keep factionalizing instead of cooperating and compromising.

Algeria has been pulling out of its baby soul perceptivity,[3] getting restive and even rioting periodically over the past few years. It is ready to create a new manifestation—when it can scoot past a wave of fundamentalist pressure. As usual when a particular strand of consciousness is about to be passed by, it often rears up and insists on asserting power. Part of Algeria wants to secularize and surge forward into the late 20th century; another part doesn't and is made exceedingly nervous at the prospect—thus the big fundamentalist turn out and win at the polls. However, neither young soul politicians nor the military were about to lose a chance for control, so they canceled democracy and placed themselves in office by fiat. Because the current of consciousness in Algeria is heading towards a strong young

---

[3] 30% baby and 32% young, plus about 23% infant.

soul future, the military will likely get away with their coup and remain in power using whatever force it takes to quash the religious right. The world's democracies actually had few mixed feelings about which was better, fundamentalists canceling democracy once they were elected, or the military beating them to it.

This nation is neither steaming towards increased consumerism nor towards a stable climate in which to do business. Among young souls in Algeria, the yearning is for glory, power and influence in their part of the world. In other words, this area is likely to become a hot spot and a major source of trouble in the Middle East. Appearing on the scene before the passage of too many years, will be a young charismatic leader who is likely to fire up the country and create a great deal of trouble on the world scene.

The nuclear threat is greatest in the Moslem areas of the world: Iran, Iraq, India, Pakistan, Algeria, Libya and the Central Asian republics of the former Soviet Union are clearly red zone danger areas. Although any use of nuclear weapons is likely to be localized, this is still not healthy for the planet. Because of average soul age (baby and young) and Islamic attitudes (shrug: whatever Allah wills), neither destruction nor environmental degradation are terribly worrying issues in these countries. Fundamentalist righteousness rarely creates either moderate behaviors or deep, ecological thinking.

Turkey is also ready to move into manifesting some young soul behaviors. Turks would like to industrialize their country, make money and get out of those 1940s brown suits. The nearby remnants of the disassembled Soviet Union may present some problems for it, for if Iran goes after them with vigor, Turkey will be forced to fight to protect its interests, though it would greatly prefer to concentrate on business and cultivating ties with the West. Earlier in this century Turkey's Ottoman Republic was about as grand as an empire has ever been, but the country was left

with no glory and little money. Because of this recent past history, Turks are suspicious of expansionism.

Morocco has done an unusual experiment in its soul age
mixture, having roughly 25% each, infant, baby, young and mature with a few old souls tossed in. Despite pervasive poverty,
this evenness among the four soul ages helps create balance, stability and a fair amount of tolerance for one another.

Egypt is evenly matched between baby and mature souls,
with about twelve-percent each infant, young, and old. It has a
strong intellectual, free-thinking tradition which helps keep it
politically stable and less prone to the waves of passionate fundamentalism sweeping the region. However, its small number of
young souls makes rational planning elusive. The infrastructure
remains shabby, the bureaucracy thick, mind-boggling and time-
consuming. Its population grows unchecked, a million more
mouths every nine months. During the difficult years to come,
Egypt, already backed into a corner, will find itself in a worsened position as far as being able to provide food or healthcare
for its people. We expect much death and disease to come this
way, along with sadness and despair. Emotional suffering oftentimes reaches wrenching peaks in mature soul areas because mis-
fortune and hardship in a community make for intense bonding
experiences—again, not anybody's idea of a good time while
suffering through it.

Afghanistan, Turkmenistan, Iran, Azerbaijan, Turkey and
Iraq will be the nations most subject to damaging earthquakes in
this area. Weather looks more extreme in all of the Middle East
and North Africa, with more hot, more cold, and generally less
frequent, more erratic precipitation.

Overall, the Middle East has the most unsettled and omi-
nous feel to it of any area in the world. People have been disgruntled for centuries, feeling that history somehow took a wrong turn
after the Crusades. Moslems want their former greatness back,
vindication seeming worth almost any price. When emotions run

this strong, thinking is not terribly clear. Arabs feel sorry for themselves, martyred, victimized by the West which paid them little respect and then pushed Israel down their throats. The severely disgruntled often have a penchant for overnight solutions. In the Middle East, this means messianic leaders with promises of glory and renewed Arab vigor.

Without a spirit of cooperation, compromise and some support from the outside world, this area may destroy itself—and possibly more. By 97 or 98, a leader much more savvy and charismatic than Hussein or Khomeini, and potentially much more troublesome for the rest of the world, will have arisen. He will no doubt be seen to have the answer for all the ills and weaknesses of the Arab world. His aim to unite all Arab nations under one banner and upend the West for good won't manifest, but the possibilities are there for an incredible amount of chaos and destruction along the way.

What appears to be the surest way to avert huge problems and potential disaster is for the West to work more carefully and evenhandedly with Arab areas, beginning now. The irritation Israel causes needs to be defused, both by reining it in and by the pursuit of more equitable policies in the area by western nations. Mired in ideology as it is, the Arab mentality encourages isolation; due to Islamic purity, and pride, Arabs are not easily won over by Western material goods, which they may want but also see as a sign of a sick world. But—and this is the saving grace—the mature soul has a knack for discerning what will support people, motivate them and bring out their best. It would be wise to apply that knack to the nations and peoples of the Middle East.

Western countries have worked covertly to destabilize many Arab countries, to keep them off balance and functioning poorly, thus causing local lives to become increasingly frustrating and impoverished. People come to realize that their playing field is tilted; the more upset they get, the more open they be-

come to the appeals of the next messianic leader with an easy, violent solution. While it is true that covert actions have kept these
countries from being as powerful or as threatening in the short
term as they might have been, this kind of activity is very costly
in the long term and usually causes considerably more bad feelings, ricochets and odd karmas than positive results. Covert activity aimed at rendering certain groups, governments or countries powerless is one more young soul influenced activity the
new mature soul majority will be coming to grips with, examining these actions with new eyes and new moral values.

This short-tempered, long-seething part of the world is
clearly exasperated at not being given a fair shake by the West.
A demoralized population hyped up by a powerful leader itching for a glorious holy war against Christians and Jews could
mean much devastation. The greatest challenge for world politics in the early mature soul era will be to include and integrate
this cantankerous group of countries into world consciousness and
commerce, thereby defusing some potentially fierce problems.

ASIA
INDIA, CHINA, ETC: MOVING TOWARDS YOUNG

Many, many Asian countries are heading towards their
young soul manifestations, South Korea being but one example of
the pressure young soul masses in Asia are applying to their ruling
elites. Koreans are insisting that their government allow more
personal and economic freedom: they want the possibilities open
for their hard work to become personal monetary success. These
young souls have rioted relentlessly to win ground, foot by foot.
Since young souls will rarely quietly stomach one more life as a
peon, these situations can get explosive if rulers do not make way
for their enterprise.

Two countries, the Goliaths of world population, are on
the boundary waters between their passing baby and upcoming
young soul phases. India and China are ready and aching to be-

come gloriously materialistic; India especially would enjoy military glory also. Each has been a traditional baby soul society for decades, with the majority of citizens simply doing what parents, elders, ancestors, peers, society and religion called for. Neither has yet exhibited much technical innovation or put business needs over baby soul, kinship-oriented bureaucracies, but they will. Despite China's vaunted turn from warlords and corrupt rule by a few rich families, it is still run by a rich, powerful elite and still has a near-impossible, multi-layered (use those back door connections if you want to get anything done) style of bureaucracy. India's officialdom and red tape, also famously stupefying, finds bureaucrats stalling on everything because they are fearful of making any decision. Corruption on all levels is accepted as a fact of life in both countries, as it is in most of Asia.

China is making its shift into young. Capitalist elements of the economy are growing and the socialist elements shrinking. State factories have become a drag on China's economy, instead of the engine they were supposed to be pushing development and prosperity. The masses, intellectuals and workers alike, are longing for democracy and personal freedom. They see democracy as the freedom the West has to make money and be individualistic; the freedom to say what you want and have it count. Worldwide, people are tending to view Western democracy as an appealing, materially successful model on which to base new societies, with the mature soul conscience wanting to throw in more social protections than previously.

The energetic, enterprising Chinese are itching to be productive, make millions of products, billions of dollars—and enjoy the prizes. When given a chance, they will be superb at nurturing their businesses. Primarily because China has so many young souls, socialism did not stunt commercial instincts as it did for many Russians. The desire to do business, to create comfortable lifestyles, is much stronger in China than any pull towards militaristic adventurism. They had enough adventure with Mao! People are biding their time and strength until key members of the old guard pass away, hopefully then allowing moderates to take over from hardliners. Few Chinese are pleased with their government's actions in Tiananmen Square but, without uselessly sacrificing more people, there is nothing to do but wait. The time for major reforms has not yet arrived. In the meantime, new opportunities to make money are continually opening up. Economic freedom is coming at a faster pace than political freedom, interestingly just the opposite of what occurred, and caused chaos, in the Soviet Union under Gorbachev.

Though several of China's frail, octogenarian leaders will likely die in 92 and 93, significant change in China will not happen rapidly. Governmental structures still look very authoritarian in 94; then severe and difficult economic times hit in 95 and 96. While people have had it with authoritarian excesses, these difficult years are, by necessity, so survival oriented that political agitation for change remains mild. Some major problems will have to do with, what else, ethnic minorities. Tibetans will, of course, continue to wrangle to get their country and autonomy back—with the world behind them in spirit, though not with sanctions or guns. Minority areas in the north and west of China will begin to stir, and over the course of the next decade will be restive and difficult for the central government to handle.

There seems to be a break coming between the poorer, less-developed areas in the west and the richer, more young soul areas of southern and coastal China. There are several possible courses of action China may take here, including dropping bombs to subdue its western provinces, but eventually, certainly within the next 20 years, we see this part of the country being split off, separated politically from China proper. This area will have much internal warfare, and at this split off point, looks as ragged as Afghanistan did in 91. Given the temper of the times, China may decide not to spend the military money needed to enforce her present whole and simply let those conflicted areas in the west go, choosing instead to invest in its own productive capacities.

Food in China will definitely be a problem—it already is. Many food shortages will be localized, based on nearby climatic doings. Peasants will not be so likely to let themselves starve first (as they were forced to under Mao in order to feed the towns), and there may be an unusual amount of agitation in the countryside. Brutally cold and windy winters will paralyze northern China in 93 and 94. Some high magnitude quakes (over 8.0 on the Richter scale) are likely in the north in 95 or 96. These are huge quakes, but because the area is neither heavily populated nor economically crucial, it will not greatly affect the country's productivity or economics. The rice belt in the South comes under stress because of dry weather and looks severely blighted during several mid-decade years.

China, unlike India, has some inclination towards rational development policies. It has a traditional respect for land, regarding it as a resource to be sustained, not plundered or abused. (Sometimes, though, large ambitious projects, especially Mao's own, unwittingly created ecological havoc.) China's leaders make sure rural populations are continually taught new (hopefully improved) agricultural techniques. Planners here have shown greater respect for their population's health and education, as well as for the health of their agricultural land, than the rulers of India, a democracy.

But of course, in a democracy you can get swept out of office for unpopular policies—as Indira Gandhi found when she suggested that all government workers with three children be sterilized. Two decades ago, the Chinese woke up to the fact that their population was unwieldy.[4] Plus, they saw an unbelievable explosion in numbers still coming at them if nothing was done. That's when the two-child policy was instituted. When years of that proved not enough to stop the onslaught of new mouths, the

---

[4] 20-percent of the world's people on seven percent of the arable land is tricky, especially if you are not rich enough to import food.

even less popular one-child laws came into effect. These family-planning moves were not presented to the populace with much discussion or civility but, nevertheless, there are now "only" about fifteen million new people to feed each year.

Fixing population in India is trickier because, as mentioned, it is a democracy. The poor, who hope their children can support them in later life, do not like to give up what they see as their only hold on security. Eventually though, as ambitious, individualistic young souls continue to be born, India's population figures will start to stabilize simply because young souls are risk takers who tend to see security not in children but in their own ingenuity. But even if India could hold its galloping birthrate to its current rate of increase, it would still surpass China's population in about 30 years—on even less arable land. As you can predict, this would be a major disaster, though it is not the likely scenario. Systems and situations won't be pushed quite that far.

Like most developing nations, neither has much of a track record in keeping pollution down, though both are seeing plenty of public health reasons to begin. China guards the health of each individual with some vigilance, while India's attitude is less careful. The well-fed, healthy person is capable of producing far more than the small cost of keeping her nourished and fit. Ignorance and malnutrition create a weaker, less productive work force, while access to clean water, doctors and education do just the opposite. Most countries heading towards young are ready to discover and apply that truth. However, feeling helpless about having too many people on too little land has numbed India to the pain of "natural" corrections, like death from famine, epidemics and unprepared-for natural disasters. It is a very different human experience to be among milling throngs competing over every tiny piece of resource, including the sidewalks, than to have too few people to "subdue" the land, as was occurring just two centuries ago. Humans like their variety in big packages; this bundle of experience though has pushed nature to its limits.

China and its freshly young soul neighbors—South Korea, Taiwan and Singapore—have accomplished the unusual over the last decade and managed to close some of the gaps between the privileged and the poor. As populations have risen over the last 30 years in typical undeveloped countries, the poor have received less and less a share of the national wealth. India follows that pattern; China does not. With poverty in India measurably worsening year by year, and disparities continuing to widen between top and bottom, the poor are being forced to scramble more frantically each year simply to stay alive.

China and India, rich culturally, but painfully poor and populous, are heading into their young soul phases very differently, and will create different effects in the world. Despite pervasive, long-term human rights offenses, China is in more integrity with its people as it heads towards a young soul expression that is both technologically inventive and happily materialistic.

India already makes more movies per year than Hollywood. With its exuberant, lavish, and lively art and music scene, it could become fantastically creative, artistic, inventive—and rich. However, because of scattered planning and top heavy distribution of wealth, it is more likely heading for trouble. Ethnic rivalry, favoritism and bitterness will continue to take a huge toll. India's internal chaos will no doubt cause a bit of external chaos with its neighbors, and quite possibly with the world at large. With newly bulging armies, India has become progressively more militaristic and inclined to push around the smaller countries which border it—Nepal, Pakistan and Sri Lanka have all felt that muscle only recently. India is having expansionistic dreams, and could well use an incursion into another country to take attention away from internal problems. Like the people of Iran and Iraq, India's educationally and nutritionally handicapped masses could, for a period of time enjoy the adventurism of their leaders. Anything which would make them feel powerful as a people could have attraction, even if it means a war in which they and their brothers may die.

Pakistan is also moving into its young soul expression, with its own set of angry feelings and expansionistic dreams. Under severe land pressure because of population and drought, it is likely to try some encroachment of its own. At the very least, it would like to have more of Kashmir, an area now mostly within India's northern boundaries.

Both India and Pakistan have nuclear weapons which they may use on each other. We see that as a 50-50 chance. The planet's newly developing consciousness has created a majority of countries that are now inclined to work together towards world peace, using diplomatic pressure and economic sanctions against the inevitable outlaws. India and Pakistan are likely to find themselves on the receiving end of these tactics.

Despite the increasing numbers and misery of its poor, India has also been adding to its middle class. City people are managing to get jobs or create businesses that pay well enough to buy consumer goods of every stripe. For the first time ever, consumer credit has been made available and large numbers of people are using it, abandoning the traditional modest savings programs most families previously maintained. Generally, of course, it is the young souls who are pushing themselves up the monetary scales—whether on credit or not—and, like the typical newly rich, view the poor with little compassion, often as cheap labor or a backward embarrassment to their country.

India's ravaged environment will worsen. These fresh young souls want their chance to get at the country's resources and are not likely to allow laws protecting the environment to come into serious enforcement. Poisons abound on land, in water and air. Agricultural soil is in terrible shape, much of it becoming desertified. Deforestation is not likely to stop despite a growing peasant-based tree-hugging movement; erosion and flooding will worsen. Water is severely short; ground water is not replenishing itself. Both mismanagement and lack of management have created a dearth of options and shrinking positive possibilities for the future.

In India we see extreme weather as the major coming assault. Hotter and dryer weather for most of the country, and then flooding wet weather as precipitation gets compressed into shorter wet seasons. Harsh, late monsoons will cut into growing seasons and cause crop losses. Severe food shortages are likely here for many years, with little hope of imports to save the day. Indians don't have terribly strong constitutions in the first place, what with pervasive calorie and protein shortages and unclean drinking water and parasites. Increased food shortages mean a further weakening of the human body, more disease and a severe reduction in the average person's productivity. Food riots based on frustration and anger at unfair distribution practices will be common in many cities. The poorest minorities will experience increased intolerance and growing pressures on them because people take out their frustrations on those furthest down the status rungs.

Laos, Cambodia and Vietnam contain primarily baby souls, though Vietnam has a nearly equal number of young souls. Southeast Asia still easily beats out Afghanistan as the most booby-trapped place in the world—mines and the exploded, unexploded and poisonous debris of war are everywhere. You cannot build healthy people or strong nations on a toxic waste dump. Weather looks as if it will become hotter and harsher in Southeast Asia, making increased disease problematic.

Thailand tends to concentrate its baby soul populations in the country, with its cities magnetizing the young and mature souls. Its city dwellers, particularly, have an entrepreneurial spirit and a strong taste for making money. Thanks to the consciousness of its people, who absolutely did not want fighting on their territory, and plain good luck, Thailand did not become embroiled in the wars of recent decades. The biggest problems we see here are health issues created by massive population increases, shrinking food supplies, high levels of HIV and AIDS and intensifying problems with tropical diseases, especially incurable malarias and leprosy.

JAPAN: YOUNG AND ON TOP

Japan is definitely enjoying its new status. People are having a wonderful time spending their money, doing it with increasing elegance and style. Its politicians are only now beginning to figure out what to do with their power and how not to bungle public relations with the rest of the world. The local, home-brewed brand of young soul corruption is already showing up more often in government, finances, business practices—and in gangs. Squeaky clean is becoming soiled.

Japan will be experiencing continual problems with environment and food supplies. It has poisoned itself with modern technologies and its young soul disregard for the environment, and like the U.S., it searches for ways to get around necessary cleanups. To take one interesting example, its ocean waters have become so polluted that not enough sunlight can get through to produce the seaweeds of which they are so fond. They are experimenting with masses of night time grow-lights focused on the seaweed banks, hoping this extra light will make up for the reduced penetration of sunlight. Of course, it can't make up for polluted seaweed, but that is not the issue, yet. While traditional Japanese food choices tend to support the health of their population, their food and environment are increasingly chemicalized with little regard for what that could mean downstream—all typical young soul goings-on.

The gravest problem with Japan, however, is that it is under great geological stress and prone to high magnitude earthquakes in the 90s. We see the likelihood of a large quake in southern Japan, near Nagasaki or Hiroshima, in 93; this looks strong, over 8.0 points on the Richter scale. Rice growing and other agriculture appears disrupted for several years. In 94 or 95, Tokyo looks like it will sustain a very devastating mid-8 point earthquake, one that causes much flooding and tidal damage. This quake puts the most industrialized country out of business for awhile. Investments around the world that can be sold quickly will be, for the Japanese will need to get their money home to rebuild. But, as they do this it causes chaos on international stock and real estate markets. Tokyo's demise is crushingly hard on the rest of the world, one more reason that these mid-decade years are so difficult.

NORTH AMERICA

The U.S. and Canada, both strong young soul countries, are now in the process of creating their mature soul expressions in the world. Canada has traditionally been more compassionate and supportive of her citizens through social programs, community services, childhood and old age safety-nets, while the U.S. has been the mightier, jazzier, more competitive place to live. It is easy to see that Canada's transition into this new consciousness era is more likely to be smooth sailing than that of the U.S., with its traditional self-reliant, pick-yourself-up-by-your-own-bootstraps mentality still in strong play. Furthermore, the U.S. will be more keenly feeling its decline as an economic powerhouse. For both Americans and their leaders, this change takes some time to assimilate. Americans must learn to partner with Japan, Europe and the U.N. and cut back on bullying to get what they want.

MINORITY LIFE

Both Canada and the U.S. have large ethnic groups which are currently calling attention to themselves, wanting bigger slices of the pie, more protections and consideration. In Quebec, the French are becoming increasingly vocal: they want more autonomy and respect from the sea of English speakers surrounding them—or they want a totally separate state; no longer will they put up with what they see as second class citizenship. In the U.S., African-Americans are too widely scattered about the country to be calling for a separate state, or surely they would. Blacks have been set aside to stew in their own juices for a long time and are genuinely angry, increasingly vocal and volatile. America seems a racist world that allows them little success. The U.S. certainly does have a strong element of racism and has, especially in the past, purposefully gone out of its way to undermine healthy black communities.

The people who have become most successful—meaning rich and respected—in North America typically have been intellectually centered, education-valuing, hard-focused, business-minded individuals who were willing to persevere against great odds; dreamers or risk-takers sometimes, but with aspirations they could logically expect to attain. The successful have come from all soul age groups, but are most often young souls themselves or the offspring of young soul parents who imprinted their children with go-get-'em values. They have come from all races and nationalities, but particularly from Northern Europe and Asia.

Blacks in the U.S. have typically been mostly baby or mature souls, without the focused drive of the young soul. African families traditionally put emphasis on the collective whole, and little emphasis on education or on individual striving for success. Blacks, consequently, have not been as well supported as Asians and Europeans have by cultural traditions to go grab success. In addition, most North American blacks have chosen to be either emotionally centered (which has helped gain success in music and acting) or moving-centered (which helped with athletics and dance). These favored centering choices do not help them swim with mainstream America.

Each lifetime before you even set foot on the planet, you decide to be either primarily intellectual, emotional or moving centered. (Also you choose a secondary center to use, with the remaining center then becoming harder to access.) Worldwide, people divide themselves equally between these three choices. Current North American culture, however, is 50-percent intellectual, 40-percent emotional and a mere ten-percent moving. Half of all African-Americans are lively, moving centered individuals who express themselves by moving and doing, which feels foreign, often even threatening, to the average, sedentary, intellectually centered white who expresses through thinking and abstract concepts.

Now, seeing that you all pick your lifetimes, why would anyone choose a black skin in a white world, an emotional or moving center in an intellectual world, and a locale where your soul age was not the main player? Challenge and growth, of course, but spending a lifetime marked by your skin color and hounded by feelings of social inferiority and anger are nobody's ideas of a good time. In fact, one reason for the attraction of drugs in black culture is that the experience of life is so much harsher and more intense than expected. Ambitious astral plans for growth through cruel trials can feel overwhelming once you are in your body on the planet. Drugs numb pain, though, unfortunately, block most growth and evolution.

Minority life has a way of being intense and difficult in most areas of the planet. Humans truly push this method of growth to interesting, unusual extremes. Being outside mainstream throws you squarely on your own resources; for one, you must either accept what the dominant culture says about you, and suffer with self-loathing, or you are forced to go against the predominant culture, think for yourself and figure alternative explanations for your predicaments. That process is strengthening; you are personally enhanced because you have explored yourself and contemplated the ordering of the universe. Because it induces doubts which require growth, plugging into a minority community experience is a recurring mature soul scenario. In North America, as elsewhere, it is an experience likely to remain potent and wrenchingly difficult.

We are not implying that because people "choose" a certain life experience, whether being a Jew in Moscow or a black in Detroit, that they will feel invigorated by their adventure or enlightened by the growth required of them. Nor are we implying that the social structures which make those experiences so formidably uphill should remain unchanged. It is your essence that chooses a difficult lifetime, not your earthly personality, which in most lifetimes would select not only the same color skin and religion as the in-charge majority, but a kindly father who owns a candy store and gives you a big red car and trust fund at age seventeen.

Sometimes it is hard to figure what in the world your essence had in mind for you. Once you are born, your personality can be upset, even horrified, about the mess it finds itself in. (When it is the *essence* that finds life unsatisfactory, it can essentially opt out within the first two years before it is strongly connected to the body. This is not difficult: Crib deaths are one manifestation of essence dissatisfaction, but so are many other more scientifically explainable deaths.) All societies incubate these kinds of minority prejudices, but these behaviors will now be under the glare of the spotlight more frequently. Most often, it is the mature soul individual who puts energy and emotion into rooting out social evils in order to make life more equitable for everybody, including themselves in future lifetimes.

TAXES

Getting the U.S., in particular, into a more equitable place is going to be interesting, very interesting. The 80s witnessed the dying "grasp" of young soul mentality. Both the Reagan and Bush administrations created widening schisms between rich and poor, and served business interests, the military and the ultra-rich to the detriment of the middle and lower classes. Deregulation, for example, opened the way for outright thefts by executives at savings and loans, with the total amount so large that it will drain 50 to 60 dollars a *month* from each American household for the next 20 *years.* Failing banks, stock trading companies, corporations and insurance companies are certain to add more to that bill. The ultra-rich have considerably more wealth than they did ten years ago; almost everybody else has less—less income to spend, less social support, less education. The numbers on paychecks may have risen, but spending power and support services for the average citizen have been diminishing since the mid-70s.

Theoretically, the Reagan windfall tax-cut for the rich was to trickle down into research, development and more factories. It didn't. Instead, it vanished into junk bonds, real estate speculation, leveraged buy-outs, art auctions, yachts and luxury automobiles, all the last grasp stuff of the 80s. America is less competitive than ever and under Reagan's leadership became first a debtor nation, and finally the largest debtor nation in the world.

Most Americans, except the already demoralized poor, don't like to admit that they are increasingly threadbare, and thus tend not to bring the issue into focus. In fact, some prop themselves up by identifying the poor class below them as the culprits who have taken their money. The public in the U.S. so strongly identifies with being well-off (or potentially well-off) that, even when they can't buy what they could last year or finance their children's educations, they are loathe to admit their status has changed. And if they can't afford to travel to Europe or Japan, they don't get the first-hand experience of being a poor cousin instead of the well-off American of recent memory, flashing greenbacks and feeling on top of the world.

Americans don't like to believe they have a class system. The working myth is that everybody could be rich if they were ambitious, smart and lucky enough (though often now all hopes are pinned on the lottery). This skewed version of reality is one reason Americans rarely consider acting in a bad-mannered way towards the rich. Hardly anybody points vigorously to the corruption of banks, savings and loans, insurance companies or stock trading companies, companies which bilked the public of astronomical amounts of wealth. Very few bother to yell: Don't tax me more; tax the rich who have the money, the social and political advantages and tax-rule favoritism.

While people grumble about taxes and politicians, they actually haven't been willing to tackle the tax structure—or the political system beneath it. It is easier to let the welfare mother remain the scapegoat, or for liberals, the Pentagon. Thinking in terms of economics seems so complicated.

The Democratic Party has been in a long crisis with little excitement going on or truth coming out. The social programs of Lyndon Johnson's era were found unworkable and too expensive, Jimmy Carter a good man but an anemic leader. Little attractive, fresh or practical emerged since, until Bill Clinton. Of course, now that the country is really broke it gets all that much more difficult (and interesting) to make needed changes.

While Canada has been easing itself into a mature expression, the U.S. has been tearing off in the opposite direction, making middle class life harder and harder to attain and maintain. The set-up in the U.S. is exquisite, at least in its ability to create upsets, drama, and social divisions in need of mending. Except for new focus the Clinton administration brings, little urgency has been felt within government to do anything about worsening poverty or the increasing collection of wealth by a few. There has been no leadership on either side of the issue, just band-aid patchwork schemes to quiet voters down and allow politicians to retain their privileged lifestyles.

While the general public is beginning to sense that environmental security may be more important than military "security", politicians are not yet willing to get too radical, especially if it means closing bases or losing jobs in their states. However, as money gets tighter in the mid-90s, people will start to zealously guard how it is spent. Unless the U.S. chooses to go bottoms-up economically, as the U.S.S.R. did to keep its huge military in place, military spending will be cut, chopped and shredded, despite the usual Pentagon threats of pending disaster. Having a big military is not a major thrill for mature souls who know intuitively that there's got to be a better way. How public moneys are spent will be analyzed endlessly; suddenly, economic restructuring is no longer "too complicated" for the average citizen, but something she has great interest in.

REDESIGNING SERVICES

The mid- to late-90s will see a truly radical economic overhaul. When money looks as if it is being misused, people will yelp, loudly and to good effect. Attention and creativity will be on fixing what is wrong with "the system". Aside from the military, the country will be reevaluating its technology-heavy healthcare system which costs an inconceivable amount for delivering so meagerly. Hard moral and practical decisions will finally get made: Bailing out premature crack babies from their first year of multiple crisis situations to the tune of $50,000 each won't be seen as a useful way to spend money, nor throwing $200,000 worth of aggressive treatment at a dying cancer patient to extend her life by a few uncomfortable months. Organ transplants may start looking too expensive also, and heart bypass surgery like a hi-tech rescue for those who haven't bothered to care for their bodies. Keeping a million Americans alive, year after year, in vegetative comas from which they have no chance of recovery won't be seen as a needed service, but extremely wasteful. Broad, general right-to-die laws are bound to be passed amid much discussion about how a person's last years and weeks should look and how much they should cost.

While mature souls like to make sure everybody is cared for, they aren't so phobic about death as the young soul who will more often hold on to life at all costs, convinced that this one body is the only chance there is. The mature soul begins to get the idea that there may be more to life than the physical body and starts to view the death process as a part of life, which is sometimes better not put off. Six years of decay, staring at the ceiling of a nursing home sounds horrifying to anyone; the young soul, though, may do it, clinging tenaciously to life. The mature soul may find letting go a more appealing action. Without denial or fear, and with a relatively clear mind there is a fair degree of control over how and when you exit.

Self-responsibility for health is a concept which will come on stronger and stronger, particularly in the already puritanical U.S. The average guy will be feeling more concerned and responsible for his own health when hi-tech fix-it money starts drying up. Television will have blatant propaganda promoting "eating right," exercising and quitting bad habits. The U.S. will likely follow California's lead and tax tobacco heavily enough to pay for hard-punching anti-smoking campaigns on television and radio. Canada already places sufficiently high taxes on tobacco products to discourage use—and encourage smuggling. (As this reprioritizing mood sets in, gasoline may finally get the tax it deserves too, one which will support conservation, public transport and leave room for the development of clean technologies.) It could be that soft drinks and sugar will receive punitive taxes in order to discourage their use also, for healthy people will be seen as an important asset, part of any country's bankable wealth.

The issues surrounding a government's ability and responsibility for providing healthcare for its citizens will be hotly discussed. What you saw in 1992's presidential campaign was but a taste of the debate to come. Expensive options will surely be rationed and deleted as more money finds its way into the areas that have high payoffs, like prenatal and preventive care and health-promoting strategies. Many Europeans enjoy easy and cheap access to homeopaths and herbalists because these non-toxic modalities work, stave off more serious problems, and are cheap. Because they make sense monetarily, the U.S. may find itself bringing these health strategies into mainstream, despite the usual opposition, the catcalls of quackery and predictions of doom from the ever-dependable American Medical Association.

As money tightens, the educational system will increasingly falter until it is redesigned with community support and participation. Education will be the hot issue of the mid-90s. How can you best train and educate children and evolve them into thriving, productive adults? Can education dare neglect children's emotional lives, their self-esteem issues, and the different ways they learn? How do you inculcate kids with positive attitudes and values—and stop crime before it starts? Americans are clear that drilling children as stressfully as the Japanese do will never work; so, what is the best way to help young people be whole and vital, and to find zest for what they do and keep the U.S. competitive? These are some of the big questions a concerned citizenry will be raising in just a few years.

The vision that comes in strong by 96 is that "we" have got to take care of each other. To do that many aspects of life must be examined freshly. By this point, the public will be in a bottom-line truth kind of mood. Politicians who dance and shuffle, or who are on the take won't last. By 96, the old guys and the old system will have hardly a leg to stand on. If Clinton survives the economic bloodbath of the next years and manages during his first term to retain his populism and his integrity, to continue consensus building, and he proves good at inspiring communal enterprise, then his reelection is quite likely. If not, people will toss him because 96 is a crucial year. This election demands a moral leader, a person of the caliber of Abraham Lincoln or Teddy Roosevelt, a person who will help the nation to clarify certain ideas in order to move forward to a more stable, wholesome future. Clinton was elected as the mature soul focal point for needed structural and attitudinal changes. If he handles himself well during his first years, then the election will be his.

Times remain difficult. The world keeps throwing boomerangs; bad luck unfortunately starts to feel normal. But this new urge to reinvent social and political life keeps these years from feeling dismal, as the years of the Great Depression did. People sense that out of their pain and hardship a new, better, more workable society is being built. The outer world gives few choices; life can't go on in the same old ways. Clearly, though, many positive changes are being forced by harsh circumstance.

EARTH AND WEATHER CHANGES, CONTINUED

In North America, we see 1994 as likely to be an exceedingly difficult year for food crops. The summer seems not to warm up, especially in the wheat, corn and potato growing midsection of the continent, with the consequence that food shortages will be rampant. Next year's harvest looks only slightly improved. The cold growing season is caused by a large amount of volcanic debris in the atmosphere, blocking sunshine and heat. (This may be from the nearby eruption of Mt. Baker or Mt. Rainier, as well as from action much further away.) The 94-95 span is the worst of the bad-weather years because so much food growing territory is adversely affected by the string of volcanic eruptions and explosions.

The next dozen years will see a startling amount of volcanic activity in the Northern Hemisphere especially. In North America, this will be occurring all the way up and down the West coast from Mexico to Alaska. California will be subject to continuing strong earthquakes, beginning as early as 1993 in the greater Los Angeles area. Two quakes with well over 8.0 force now looks odds-on, with substantial widespread flooding, property damage and loss of life. Even in a well-prepared area, these are monster quakes that no one dusts off from easily.

Santa Barbara, Sonoma and the Hayward fault area of Northern California are other major hot spots in the state, but quakes in these locales will mostly range in the more survivable mid-seven range of the Richter scale.

Oregon, Washington, Idaho, British Columbia and Alaska will see increasing earthquake activity as well as a troublesome increase in volcanic activity. The Boston/New York area also sits on increasingly strong stresses. It is likely to be hit by intense, damaging earthquakes, probably in 96, though possibly a year or two later.

In general, it is the coastal areas of the U.S., Canada and Mexico that are subject to the most frequent difficulties. The West coast and the Gulf coast, including the Florida Keys, are particularly vulnerable. Coastal areas are usually highly populated simply because they are active, alive, attractive places to live. That they are more dangerous does not mean every piece of coastline will be quaked, flooded or nearly blown away.

In the early 1800s, the New Madrid fault, which runs along the Mississippi Valley, spawned the mightiest set of earthquakes (8.6 Richter) ever in the U.S. The fault is stressed again, and active. While it is too unsettled to forecast clearly what will happen, this fault will likely stay relatively quiet for the rest of the decade and then achieve a grand release early in the new century. New Madrid is a dangerous fault not only because of the thousands of square miles it can so easily adversely affect (from Louisiana to Illinois and over to Pennsylvania), but because most Midwestern towns have few protective measures against earthquake damage written into their building codes or consciousness.

WESTERN EUROPE
Western Europe has the largest enclaves of mature and old souls now on the planet and thus naturally tends to be at the forefront of social change. In many ways, this area will be more comfortable simply because it has already successfully put much of the new social agenda into action. France, Germany, Italy, England, Denmark, Finland, Sweden and Norway have high pro-

portions of mature souls in their populations, high taxes and kindly governmental policies, as does Holland with its high proportions of old souls. Germany and Greece have matching numbers of mature and baby souls. Switzerland used to be old, but is fast becoming more young-influenced. Belgium and Austria are gradually winding down their young soul phases, while Spain is newly, arrogantly, young and Portugal still stalwartly baby.

Mature souls usually feel it is important to support each other and help the underdog, so guaranteed health and welfare services are generally found—at least in the richer nations. Europeans also support mental and creative health by making four to six weeks paid time off mandatory every year for all workers, including nannies and maids still new to their jobs. Europeans have a hard time understanding how anyone can keep a family or a soul together on one or two weeks of annual vacation, a quandary you old souls can surely identify with.

Europeans also ponder how the U.S. allows so many homeless people to exist, much less starve or freeze. And, hearing about families being bankrupted by medical expenses sounds like a medieval horror story. To them, communal action to provide social safety nets for each citizen seems the only right, morally responsible, self-respecting way to proceed.

Some mature soul European nations have a gentle, grandmotherly feel to them which sets an example for the rest of the world about how life can work. With experience, these countries have become more sophisticated (and realistic) in their handling of health care, social programs and educational systems. There will be agonizing here as consumer lifestyles disappear, but people will rapidly become involved in trying to make life work within the new parameters. Europeans will experience less panic when facing survival issues than North Americans. They will quickly adjust as necessary and be ready to assist others, including others outside of Europe, even when money and food are short—well, except for encouraging immigrants. Europeans absolutely do not want a flood of economic or environmental refugees making chaos out of what they have so painstakingly put together and will do their best to protect themselves from any such onslaught. While they might like to fix the world, they know realistically that they cannot.

Ethnic ties and mature soul morality pushed Germans toward reunification. Economic and social costs have been high but seem worth it, even to the suddenly less-rich West Germans faced with their thankless cousins. The underlying conviction is that whatever the burdens, and however intense the changes, it was the one right thing to do. Germany greatly needs to tackle, head-on, its current batch of ethnic and race issues. If it does not defuse the hatred and vengeance against poor immigrant groups, that hostility and incipient Naziism will sap the country's strength and eat at its heart.

Nations with strong agricultural components, like Britain and France, will be in better shape than those that must import food, like Belgium and Holland, although those two both manage to scrape through the decade not too badly scathed. The Scandinavian countries look too cold for several of the mid-decade years, much chillier in the summer too, which interferes greatly with food production. Scandinavia has the worst problems with increased cold weather, though much of Europe will be lashed by fierce, mid-decade, rain and snow storms.

Spain and Greece are apt to be short on water, hotter and more droughty than usual. Spain falls back into poverty, but having only recently come out of extreme poverty, it is easier to deal with. By mid-decade, Italy looks shaken by volcanoes and quakes of a very serious nature. Earthquake activity is also strong in Greece and Cyprus. Nature will be hitting these countries intensely, causing economic and social difficulties and extreme food shortages. Italy becomes very chaotic and is likely to be the most uncomfortable place in Europe.

Overall though, the weather looks reasonably benign in

Western Europe and growing seasons usually manage to reap fair harvests. Decent weather helps most European countries hold together fairly well during these trying years. Economics aren't great, but still better than in most places.

EASTERN EUROPE

This is the largest, most obvious place where young soul dirty habits are coming face to face with mature soul consciousness. Environmental concerns were what first rallied people together in many Eastern European countries, thus inadvertently creating the power bases from which the dictators were later toppled. Eastern Europe is exceedingly poor, rundown, and dreadfully polluted. Though the post revolution present is harsher than anyone imagined possible, many people nevertheless feel positive about the future, and full of possibilities.

When a country draws tight ethnic boundaries or lets old resentments rise up and rule, its economy and infrastructure go to hell, wars start, people die and life gets increasingly intense and uncomfortable. For most Eastern European countries this would represent a regressive descent into young soul chaos, where everybody fights viciously for a bigger piece of the pie, clearly not a winning situation. In Rumania and Yugoslavia, the only uniting factor for most groups of people was opposition to the old leader, not a clear vision of improved life for all. These are the two countries most likely to continue to indulge ethnic disharmony, and skid further downhill.

These two East European countries serve as a laboratory where the Western world, most especially the former Soviet republics, can see by blatant, horrific, example what happens when people allow this plunge into confusion and internal fighting. Eastern Europe also models for the world what creativity and goodwill can create—with the perseverance of Job and some knowledge and investment from the rest of the world.

Rebuilding after the dictatorships is not easy. Redoing

your foundations, whether after a mud-slide, fire, war or governmental collapse, is rarely a favored, first-choice activity, but it is
exciting and involving. It forces you to let go of your past and
to think carefully about what you want to build. Will you join
forces, synergize, communicate, create together and move
through grim times strengthened? Or will you fight and fall into
anarchy, wars and devastation? One way you fly; the other leads
to increasing impoverishment.

In Czechoslovakia, Poland and Hungary, creativity and a
fair amount of outside help is starting to create rich potentials
and nice open futures. In Rumania, Bulgaria and Albania, all
heavily weighted with baby souls and the tenacious greed of
many of the same young souls who previously wielded power,
governments have remained authoritarian. Mature consciousness
is not strong enough to get these three moving in new, exciting
ways; simply put, there isn't the people power to make large
scale change.

Yugoslavia is due to break itself into at least three separate
chunks, which, peace measure or not, will cause a fair amount of
chaos. For one, many people must then decide whether to move
behind newly created borders in order to be with their ethnic
group or dare staying put in the towns where they are rooted.
New borders and peace agreements aside, this area will remain
potentially volatile for some time, and will have trouble even
creating a stable base for agriculture.

Volatile ethnic disputes are the social downside of mature
soul existence, but they do bring up for examination, in grueling
detail, what happens when two peoples refuse to let go of the past
to find mutual common sense, compromise and some compassion for each other. Yugoslavia also exemplifies the danger of
succumbing to baser instincts and pushing to the top, like the
Serbs have, a tough, young soul leader whose mind doesn't en-
compass win/win solutions.

THE FORMER SOVIET UNION

As political, military, economic and legal structures fall apart, many new experiences will come to life, and many new social experiments be ushered in—some more consciously designed than others. Life in Russia, as in most of the former republics, is full of chaos and agony, with pain and worry everywhere, yet underneath all of that, relief exists and still some sense of excitement. The heavy mature and old soul influence makes these former Soviet areas act and react uniquely to the new set of problems.

Russia itself, the Baltics, Mensk, Ukraine, Georgia and Armenia are full of mature and old souls, now often emotionally drained and full of complaints. People feel overwhelmed with the number of changes that need to be made, but there exists a powerful backbone feeling which insists: We are strong enough to handle this and to create more interesting, fulfilling ways to live. The problem is that no one really knows, for sure, that they can actually accomplish anything of the sort. People are hardly daring to give voice to their hopes and longings.

In Eastern Europe many people are in a hurry to make money and industrialize, with the young souls among them pushing everybody along and creating the new values. The Chinese have such a strong young soul element that entrepreneurial fantasies and visions of material glory are running wide and high, making many people's moods fairly high too. In contrast, most areas in the former Soviet Union have little of that ambitious young soul element to push them into action. Instead, they get depressed (mature) and thoughtful and inward (old), but are not rushing around trying to make a rich future happen. Once they have felt their way through the current situation and have a course more fully in mind, they will feel more empowered and secure.

The Baltic states will remain fairly stable as will most of the European republics. Except for the very cold Northern Hemisphere years of 94 and 95, food growing conditions in this area actually improve. The Ukraine and Georgia, already fertile grain growing areas, appear to remain in good shape weather-wise, politics being unfortunately a trickier matter..

Many of the former Central Asian republics are on a slow slide towards social chaos, fighting and/or authoritarian regimes. These areas are primarily Islamic and are bound to be attracted to some of the fundamentalist tenets and drama of the Middle East. Rich in resources and baby souls, but not in education, technology or development, we see the probability of strife in these areas as strong. People here are less decided on which way to go and what to do than in Russia itself, where at least there is a clear determination to build a secure and unique society.

The republics adjoining Turkey and Iran—Georgia, Armenia and Azerbaijan—will be in for the most problematic times. These areas are also very vulnerable to strong earthquake activity, which may quiet their internal wranglings, temporarily. Turkmenistan, which borders Afghanistan and Iran, and Tajikistan, which shares the Farsi language with Iran, are both likely to be wooed by Iran and either seduced or overpowered. China may try moving into the three republics which neighbor it, but would have trouble holding on as local sentiment is too strong against it; ultimately, China is likely to be giving up territory on its west, not expanding it.

AUSTRALIA, NEW ZEALAND & INDONESIA

Overall, Australia and New Zealand will be among the easiest places to live in the world. Weather changes won't be as severe in the Southern Hemisphere, and population, poverty and disease aren't as problematic as in Latin America. Nevertheless, both countries will be subject to some extreme weather, with Australia particularly experiencing more drought, increasing desertification and harsher ocean borne storms. Australia will also be subject to some unusual earthquakes in the North. Both nations will remain solid, socially and politically, however rough times get.

Australia, because it has large numbers of strong-spirited, practical young souls, will manage well and keep business together much longer than one might expect in such a world-dependent economy. However, plagues of grasshoppers and a pervasive grain disease in 1995 or 96 will cause food shortages, increased health problems and death, the mismanaged and degraded environment being a good part of the problem. Psychologically, Australians revert easily to a hardy-pioneer mind-set, which makes hardships seem less onerous because they are tackled with high spirit as interesting challenges.

New Zealand remains something of a safe haven, an oasis from the world's storms. New Zealanders are primarily mature, with nearly as many baby souls, both full of old-fashioned friendliness and community orientation. They will watch out for each other, emotionally and physically, in all the ways that they can. Crops and weather look as if they do amazingly well here, helping keep community spirit high; this despite problems with ultraviolet radiation. Lack of protection from the ozone layer is a big issue this far south, and will cause increasing health problems as well as problems with the numerous grazing animals here.

With its dozens of islands, Indonesia is a mixed bag. Though primarily a baby soul area, it has many areas that are moving towards young. Bali is primarily mature, with a strong old influence, and looks very stable and lucky. In the areas surging towards young soul majorities, Indonesians will use any provocation, including harsh economic times, to overthrow oppressive leaders, get land reform and gain other opportunities. Japan and the little dragon countries may be these people's success models, but political upheaval here will lead to pandemonium and destruction, not increased wealth in the short term.

The hot seasons in this area get hotter and longer, the storms more ferocious and damaging. Volcanic activity increases and earthquakes will be frequent, but the rice crops continue to be brought in, most of the time.

ANTARCTICA

The volcanoes under this continent are now active, but show no obvious steam or lava because they are deeply buried under ice over one mile thick. This current activity is but another symptom of the worldwide increase in geological activity. The problem here is that much of western Antarctica's ice, while hinged to the continent itself, lies as a thick sheet hanging over the ocean. If volcanic activity melts or violently disrupts the ice sheet's hold on the continent, watch out because sea levels will rise significantly as the ice falls free.

We see the likelihood of a major chunk breaking away in the next two decades at a little less than 20-percent probability, but this ice shelf is so immense that the part which could become unhinged would raise ocean levels twenty feet, an absolutely devastating occurrence for all low-lying and coastal areas—the very areas which shelter the majority of the world's people. Every coastline would be radically changed by such an increase; the world's many delta areas, such as Egypt's fertile and populated Nile region, or a good part of Louisiana or most of Bangladesh, would be swamped. (If the entire ice sheet were to melt, say from global warming, the rise would be nearly 200 feet!)

The predicted, extremely oceanic map of the world so many people are visualizing, we see to be a result of what happens should the ice shelf of Antarctica collapse, not the result of violent earthquakes causing California, Japan and so on to submerge, create great waves and raised seas. Again, at present, we see this Antarctic occurrence as improbable, but possible, though it unquestionably makes living on the coasts more like living on the edge than usual. This scenario would certainly be a loud way for Gaia to insist, Let's rethink—and reinvent—everything.

CHAPTER 6

Placing Yourself
Staying Put or Moving On

Altogether elsewhere, vast
Herds of reindeer move across
Miles and miles of golden moss,
Silently and very fast.
—*W.H. Auden*

Ya gotta live somewhere.
—*motto for Cleveland suggested by Jimmy Brogan*

THE OLD SOUL ADVANTAGE

There is both a skill and an art to placing yourself so that, come what may, you feel "sourced", nurtured and energized by the locale you have chosen. Here you can more easily maintain your center and do the work you are intending to do. In this chapter, we want to set you in motion, sorting through your present situation, your desires and fears, in order to get you into the right place with the right people for these upcoming changes.

Paradoxically, there is little chance of finding yourself in the "wrong" place! By doing your homework, though, you can know that you have chosen, and are not stuck. Whether you ultimately stay where you are or move on, it is helpful to look at alternatives and to acknowledge your deepest desires. Each of you will sort this material through in your own way, until you latch on to the set of options which feels aligned with the flow of your own life.

Old souls generally have the greatest versatility in deciding whether to stick with or change any given situation. While they don't usually have the large incomes or savings that make moving easier, they do have the psychological flexibility to re-think their lives and adjust to changes in place, relationships and lifestyles with some degree of ease. Baby souls usually won't have the nerve to pick up and go, unless everyone else already is, as in the wake of a severely deteriorating situation. While young souls tend to have a fair amount of money, which simplifies moving around, they are more likely to be plugged in to making it just where they are. While mature souls tend to be perceptive enough to realize trouble is brewing, they are also the people usually most committed to existing friendships, support groups and so on, and feel the most grief upon separation. Not surprisingly, it was mature and old souls who formed a huge proportion of the Jews who left Germany—and Europe—pre-1940, before life got dangerous. There were years of warnings of what was to come, but most Jews waited until they could only escape by leaving everything behind or until they could not leave at all.

Regardless of soul age, there are two common reactions individuals experience on realizing that their geographical area may become stressed or less safe. The more usual is denial. The other is the urge to flee, to ensure survival by moving to an area presumed more safe. Both these reactions are fear-based. There is, of course, no escape from fear. Whether you stick your head in the ground or run away, life tends to get worse. The first item on the agenda, therefore, is to deal with your basic fears about life and death and change.

Some of you will find it useful to fantasize and write down your own worst-case scenarios, doing this with a Buddha-like sense of detachment surrounding you. Later you can dissolve those mental pictures and bring in your humor; first it is good to know what you are dealing with internally. No place in the world is perfectly safe and secure. Bolting for Kansas or New Zealand won't necessarily guarantee safety—you can always get hit by a tornado or truck, or a faulty prediction! Furthermore, maybe you'd regret not being a major player in the excitement and adventure likely to occur in the more hard-hit areas of the world.

MORE THAN SAFETY

What we want to examine here is how you can find the place or places in the world where you most belong, where you could put down roots and feel at home. If you are content where you live now, chances are good that you may already be ideally situated. But, many, many people in just those areas we see as most prone to serious problems are restless, often experiencing inner foment, perhaps even a longing to be gone from where they are, but without clear reasons why. Sometimes, this inner push for change comes on as a strange boredom with work, work which was previously gratifying, or perhaps it is experienced as a sense of completion or even of boredom with friends and neighbors. Some people develop a pervasive sense of anger about pollution in their area or frustration with the increasing number of people and hassles. All these types of feelings are often messages you are receiving from your essence telling you it is time to move on.

It is most joyful to be living in a place and situation where you have feelings of comfort, inspiration and easy, deep connections with people. When you settle, you want to know you have found a source place for you, a healing place, come what may. Optimally, you want to be able to say to yourself: I have made my peace here. I am willing to go if this goes. I feel protected here, I know I have work to do here, and I'm not going to worry myself over the future.

You all need to answer this where-to-be question, individually as well as on a family/relationship basis. Notice what degree of comfort you have where you currently live. Do you feel secure there? How much do you enjoy it? Are you connecting with nature, feeling in touch with the Earth below your feet? How is the quality of your day-to-day life? Do you feel supported by your relationships, by the people you meet, by your city's ability to resolve its problems and issues? Is your growth assisted in a beneficial way by your area, or do you notice life is grating on you more and more?

If you remain in San Francisco only because you can make a bundle, but hate the fog, the noise and traffic, and you are no longer cheerful enough to relish the views, charm or culture, it is probably wise to move on. If the hook is money, but all the rest of you is uncomfortable, it is time to do some serious thinking and clarify your values. Generally, an old soul will come solidly down on the side of quality of life, of which money is a part but far from a totality.

DISCOMFORT MEANS FIX SOMETHING

Some people will immediately recognize feelings of discomfort in their current location. Perhaps they have heard talk of what may come in the 90s and, on a gut level many of those predictions ring true. Maybe it no longer feels right to be on the East Coast, or in a big city with potential for great stress. Maybe you have been longing for a simpler, greener life anyhow. Once you know where you want to go, you are likely to find a way to get there. If all these issues have floated up into your consciousness, most likely it is important, on an essence level, for you to get moving.

While many people may feel uneasy because of the potential for unpleasant change, some are attached to their current area because they have always been there, because their parents, relatives, all their friends, their whole alive-and-thriving support group is right there. If this is you, intensely involved where you are, but with a worrying ear out towards the future, you may want to start talking with your group about what you are sensing. Put out feelers and see who responds. You may be surprised to find others with similar concerns and leanings. Make the potential for great change in the 90s a high priority subject of discussion.

It may be that the part of your group which actually means the most to you has been aware of prospective changes and problems. These friends may have toyed with the idea of making changes, but never really allowed the thoughts much room because of the seeming impossibility of moving their whole lives somewhere else. Now you have created fresh openings and possibilities, for yourself and for the people who are so much in your heart. At the very least, discuss potentials like food or energy shortages, rough economic situations which may make mortgages or nursing homes or college suddenly too expensive to manage. This way, you can think about how you all might be able to support each other. Be creative in looking for options. Preparing in the manner which makes sense for you, whether it is finding gas shut-off valves, storing survival food, learning to garden, or taking a Red Cross or herbal medicine class will help make you more comfortable with a decision to remain.

YOUR CROWD

It is not wrong to get hints, outer or inner, that there may be trouble in your city or geographic area and choose not to make a move. Being involved with people is crucial to almost everyone. People nurture and love you, and you them. They can also drive you crazy; and they can be karmic, another major reason you may not want to leave.

Karma allows humans to experience both sides of every

type of behavior. It means cause and effect, so, for example, if you once abandoned your wife and three young children for a life of adventure, you are sure to be at the opposite end of that scenario, with that very person leaving you to fend for the children and mend your pride. Karmic relationships allow you to experience the discomfort of being treated in just the way you treated the person with whom you are now locked into this intricate tango.

Typically, an experience that took ten years at its inception will take ten years to wind up so that both parties feel complete in Earth intensity and time. Though paying back a karma (which is the side the old or mature soul is usually on) doesn't usually make anyone feel full of free will, it is generally quite compelling, intense and interesting. People who are ready to move generally aren't leaving unfinished karmas behind! On an essence level, you want to get those relationships wrapped up no matter what it takes. So, you stay or you take them with you.

Sometimes we see old souls, especially, in uncomfortable, awkward or awful relationships long after the karma has been wrapped up. Many have sensed they must have been completing karma and have even felt they must "owe" their partners for something. With the responsibility of completing karma in the forefront of their mind, they fail to sense when it is over and dutifully keep hanging around. How do you know karma is over? When the intensity suddenly drops out and the situation no longer eats away at you. While karma is going on you may knock your head against a wall, angry at yourself that you don't seem to have the guts to leave an unpleasant or even abusive relationship. But the truth is that you probably can't leave yet and still be complete. So you stay and hate your weakness.

When a karma is done, you can feel it go "clunk". You feel the shift, something has changed. Often someone is out the door fast. People also choose to stay together once karma is done because life is more comfortable then, and they can finally arrive at a sense of peace with each other. But overstaying out of a sense of moral duty or habit is often overdoing it and can cause more misery and karma.

Interacting with the group of people you've gathered around you is usually one of the primary reasons you find yourself on the planet. If you feel like staying in order to be with them, it is a much sounder old soul reason to stay put than money. If you feel free to leave your current area, you are likely to be drawn to a new area which holds many "old" friends for you, and probably for the partners and children you bring along with you.

UNBELIEVABLE?

Most parts of the United States, Canada and Australia have been so protected and so lucky that it is hard for the average citizen to imagine that life could change fast and get very tough. Europeans, with a lot more living history beneath them and two recent wars on their territory, know in their bones that security can go out the window, overnight.

Thus it is not surprising that there are many people who can't possibly admit that a serious problem could present itself. The old souls in this group will tell you quickly that if there is a problem they know they are protected anyhow. If this is you, it is good to check in with yourself to see if you actually feel well protected where you are, or are you playing ostrich? If denial may be coming up fast for you, we suggest looking a bit more deeply, for usually you will find buried fears, resignation and can't-do attitudes. It doesn't matter so much what you decide to do, but getting conscious lays the best groundwork for good decisions. Stoicism, or fortitude and dispassion, have a place in the 90s, but feeling resigned up front is not a powerful attitude and is therefore best examined.

Some people react to the potentials of the 90s with total denial. Nothing is happening and nothing is going to happen, period. They sneer about how an economy always goes up and down, the environment is fine and the Earth isn't acting up any more than usual. Generally these people won't shift from this position, even if you talk their ears off. They often set their chins and pull in their necks. If they are still feeling communicative they may tell you about someone who got scared ten years ago and sold her close-to-the-fault property and for what? Property values roared up and nothing has happened. If you are reading this book, you probably don't find yourself in this category, and you likely realized long ago that you can't change some people's opinions no matter what tactics you take.

TIMING VS. LOGIC

As far as timing a move, you manage that best by being aware of your feelings as well as what you see as your logical options. Logic will often tell you to give yourself two or three years to plan and prepare for a transition of this magnitude. Make it as painless as possible; but also watch your body and feelings for timing clues.

When the area you live in feels dense, when it doesn't feel good any more, when it feels less life-supportive than it once was, you are getting an alert. Do you notice anxiety leaves you when you are out of town, or that you get noticeably heavy or depressed coming back into town? These are signals to watch for. Acknowledge these messages, and when they get strong enough, or oppressive enough, you will go. Bury these signals, because they are inconvenient to your current plans, and you bury your sensitivity. You become dense. Your body may get sick or depressed and perhaps you stop enjoying the sunlight as it flickers through tree leaves. Now, you never notice it.

Of course, sometimes people are lucky, timing is easy and perfect. You realize you want to go, the new place which draws you is obvious, work opens up easily, good-byes are simple, and off you go.

WHERE TO?

Often you know already what area to put yourself into. Perhaps you have always wanted to go to Florida, or back to Colorado, or are being drawn to the cowboy thing—or a spiritual group—in Montana, or your parents are still in Iowa, which feels more charming every time you visit. Many of you will already have openings to walk through into your new lives, places you think about that feel magic or special or light—despite your logic which says Iowa is boring, Montana too dismal, and Colorado too rich and too redneck.

Special feelings often linger for places where you have had pleasant past lives; your body still feels especially peaceful in those locations. Also you will be drawn to climates which are your favorites from past lives and which agree with your constitution now. You may be drawn by the sacredness of a piece of land, whether in Hawaii, near the Rockies or down by the old mill stream. And you will be drawn to places because you have business there, or a person you need to meet. Sometimes it is the old gang awaiting you, a very nice scenario.

What if you are sick-and-tired, itchy-footed, and otherwise complete where you currently are, but don't have a clue about where to go next? And you can't imagine any place in the U.S. as fabulous or even very interesting. Perhaps you imagine nothing is affordable? If this is the stuff of your mind, it is important to open all its windows to new possibilities. Do not limit yourself by what you now think and know.

For instance, many Californians feel that no place else but California is decent because of the consciousness, the climate, or both. People on the East Coast indulge a more intellectual snobbery, believing that no place else could be stimulating or cultured enough. These are valid lifestyle concerns. However, when you look deeper, you may find provincialism, illusion and your ego lurking in these ports. Also, be aware that the quality of life on both coasts changed greatly, generally to life's detriment, over the last decade. You can probably sense that for yourself. Many inland areas, which formerly were boring, stagnant, provincial, dull and small-minded, have a new energy and life seeping into them, both from people and from nature itself, while the coastal areas are looking worn and no longer have the same energetic vitality as previously.

Usually people are willing to make tradeoffs when they are truly ready to change locales. Exchanging year-round warmth of climate for year-round warmth of community may start to feel like trading up, not defeat. Lamenting the loss of an excellent daily newspaper and a vital cultural scene may taper off when you have nature, safety and kindness around you.

When you begin casting about for where you belong, ask for dreams, for chance, for luck, for guidance, for inspiration from your wiser friends on the astral, your guides, Jesus, or Gaia. And then listen. Be receptive to what information and synchronicity comes your way. And, check it out. Validate for yourself what rings true, what seems exciting and right, and what seems nuts.

Most of you are sensitive enough to be able to clear your minds, and then, with the idea of finding the next perfect place to live, put your fingers to a map and see what "feels" alive and good. You will probably be embarrassed doing this, but just notice what your sensations are. What stands out? Does your heart feel good over the Rockies or near the Mississippi? Do your fingers warm and twinkle over the Southwest? Does an area seem to be magnetizing you? Be assured that being meditative and sensitized this way is considerably more helpfully tuned to inner guidance than throwing darts at the map.

HOW TO?

Sort through your possibilities with common sense, research and by making trips. If you feel strongly drawn to Tibet, and always have, we'd say call it pleasant past life memories. Read books, look at photographs, do some past life regressions, but don't spend much time considering how to make it your next domicile.

If, for example, you are considering Colorado and New Mexico as potential new centers for your life, but don't know which or where, do some research. Check out the library's specific books on those states as well as more general books like *Places Rated Almanac* and *Retirement Places Rated.* As you browse through these resources, be aware of your intuitions and feelings. It is easier to focus yourself in this way than it is to travel all over these states.

In addition to the bookish route, start talking with friends and acquaintances about their experience of those states. A town loved by somebody you love may be just the ticket you need. Listen to people's voices as they describe places. When a person really likes a certain location, his voice will glow, as may his words while he shares the memory of it with you. Then notice if you are being touched. Are you being nourished by the energetics of that spot, even through someone else's memory? By following those rays of affinity for a particular place, you end up where you want by letting your guidance lead you. If every time somebody mentions Boulder or British Columbia you sense magic, you owe it to yourself to check it out. See how it feels—in person with your feet on its ground.

It isn't wise to go to Iowa because you think it will be safe, if when you are there it feels terminally boring, you grow depressed and your body seems to weigh thousands of pounds. Safety isn't enough reason to go through that, and you can bet that isn't where your old gang is either!

When you are searching out your destination, keep your mind very open. Anything is possible. You could make a life anywhere. By staying open to all possibilities you don't limit yourself. If you love Santa Fe, or Hilo, more than anywhere on Earth, but dismiss it as non-affordable, maybe you have just lost the most wonderful place and lots of wonderful people. If the place is right, you can find a way to be there. But perhaps there is a "better" place for you; you have to use your intuition to feel this through for yourself, and not get limited by the first thoughts and objections your rational mind throws up.

It is good to gather statistics for an area. Check out the soil fertility and growing season, the levels of air and water pollution. What is the crime level, and how about the health of the educational system? Check on what the climate has been doing, and the economy, but remember it is difficult to predict with perfection what will be happening five years from now, what climatic changes or increased economic difficulties will bring to a particular area. You can't totally protect or insulate yourself from these changes, though you can make some educated guesses, such as that small will be more comfortable than big. The idea is to go with your instincts, your heart and your mind.

If you adore the area around Tucson and feel pulled to be there, but your mind says, "terrible water problem and too hot," we'd say think about it, feel it through for yourself, listen to your deepest intuition. It could be the Tucson climate will change and get better, not worse. Or, maybe you go there, meet a gang of old pals and head for Manitoba together. It is all individual, and you are best and luckiest when led by your deepest guidance. That doesn't mean throw your supposedly rational mind out, but put it in perspective by giving your intuitions, feelings and desires a good hearing. We wouldn't suggest ruling out any area you think you want to be in.

ASK FOR INSPIRATION
Work with divination. Pray, ask for guidance. Ask for clear signs about what to do or where to go. Consult the I Ching. Have a tarot reading. As you go to sleep, ask for clear, inspired dreams to show you what to do. Get some channeling.

We often rate for people how much they and their families are in affinity with a particular area, checking to see what it looks like on an emotional basis, a physical basis, a spiritual basis or on a financial basis, and rating a place for its mate-finding potential is not an uncommon request. Some of you might want to learn to use a pendulum or figure out how to use muscle testing (Applied Kinesiology) to track down this kind of information for yourself. These are both good ways to get past your mind and access your body's innate wisdom.

It is always important to validate channeling or any information you divine for yourself with your inner knowingness: information will resonate with your core energy when it is good. You feel the "click". An advantage of channeling is that it can open you up to possibilities you wouldn't ordinarily consider and ideas that represent a whole new way of thinking about your life. An advantage of working with ritual, guides, dreams, the pendulum or muscle testing, etc., is that your intuition quickens and grows as you learn to read yourself.

CHECKING OUT THE NEW LOCALE

There is a certain breed of people who are inclined to sell nearly everything, jump into a large motor vehicle, and start driving around the country trying to figure out just where they want to live or "retire". This usually ends up quite confusing, since there is so much input and so little focus. That is why we push doing homework first, getting your guidance. Wait until you have some clicks, then investigate.

Aside from all the ways you would normally size up an area, we suggest paying particular attention to your body and to your interactions with the locals. Your body will tell you if it is happy in an area by how it feels. Is it suddenly thrilled to be breathing? Is it sparkling, more upbeat than usual? Is it relaxing easily, is your first chakra content and quiet? Are you feeling nurtured by the scenery, whether natural or man-made? When the land looks beautiful and your body feels well, usually you are in a benign spot, probably one with healing energies for you. If you think everything seems pretty and OK but your body feels edgy and details are not coming together easily, you are probably not yet in your perfect place.

Notice the local people, because you will want a group of them to fill your life with all that humans can. Survey the newspapers, the bulletin boards and the yellow pages. Explore the bookstores, the health practitioners, the natural food stores, the art and music scene, the restaurants and whatever else interests you. Tell people you are interested in the area and are checking it out, trying to figure if it is where you want to be. Let them tell you how it is for them. Talk to the old-timers; talk to the supermarket clerks. Are you connecting?

When you are in an area which is right for you, you will notice you are looking into many peoples' eyes and enjoying their energy. That is one clue that you have old friends there, which always means more comfort and familiarity.

OLD SOUL ENCLAVES

Many of you will be drawn to areas where old souls are collecting, for having a generous number of somewhat like-minded individuals around you is attractive, helps smooth your life, makes socializing more fulfilling and makes it easier to feel a part of the new community.

You want to feel inspired with this move, not like a poor dog with its tail tucked in. It is crucial to feel positive about where you are going (or where you are), so even if an area is loaded with people of similar consciousness, pay attention to how well you are actually feeling and actually connecting with the individuals you meet.

There are a number of areas in the U.S. and Canada that are drawing fair numbers of old souls which seem to have a fair degree of security. The Southwest has become a major magnet. New Mexico, Colorado, parts of Utah and Arizona—people are being strongly drawn to those states. Portions of Oklahoma and

Arkansas have become attractive, as have certain areas in the Virginias, the Carolinas and Kentucky. Vermont and New Hampshire are again drawing much old soul attention, and seem comfortable havens. Montana, Minnesota and Wisconsin are noticing old soul influxes also. Along with the interior valleys of British Columbia, these are the places in North America we see with the most current old soul attention focused on them, which are also likely to remain comfortable, unwearying places to live.

While there are many other places in the U.S. which are also safe and stable or have interesting populations and all, we've only listed here the areas which are both drawing large numbers of conscious people and have a settled, balanced feel to the land.

THE FAMILY PACKAGE

If you have children, we suggest considering them, their school system, community crime levels and whatever, as well as their input, to the level which seems right to you. Your kids will instinctively be directing you away from places wrong for them and towards locales where they will be comfortable. They do not do this consciously, or even so much through their grumpiness or excitement, but they do it on an energy level, in a manner quite difficult to pin down and describe with precision.

It is not necessarily their objections that will tell you where to go or not go, because on a conscious level they do not know. Often they will object to any change, except maybe those sounding glamorous, like Malibu—or Paris. If some place is absolutely 100 points off the Richter Scale wrong for them, you probably won't be considering it long. Their unspoken energy will close the door on certain areas.

The family is a unit which moves through life together as a package—at least for as long as it stays together. Your children knew it was a package deal, that they got you, your mate or mates, your lifestyle, foibles and strengths, and they got your potential changes when they signed on and climbed aboard. They knew the parameters they would be working within. If you are choosing what to do carefully and with respect for your family, it is probably right to trust your choices even though the children may be grumbling loudly.

YOUR KIDS PICK YOU

Generally, child agreements aren't made unless everything jells on a deep level so that each essence, parent and child, gains. By that we mean that each gets the lessons it wants for growth, and is able to meet the people it needs in order to have the sets of experiences it desires. This can mean a childhood where the musical talent you want to explore gets nurtured because your dad is with the symphony and your mom plays drums in a women's rock band. It can mean a warm, supportive family, or a favored older brother who tortures and easily one-ups you. It can mean always having good old friends around you, or it can mean feeling so much like a stranger in a strange land that you are forced to explore your inner world and miss out on street-corner fun.

Your child picks you for exactly who you are and for what you are likely to offer; and you them. All this is planned on the astral plane with the sense that it will allow each person to accomplish what she wants. Again, we are not talking about idealized, trouble-free existence, but real life with warts and challenges. Generally, old souls are wrapping up karmas with their relationships including those with children, not instigating new ones. This does not mean that if you have a temper and a tendency to hit and be nasty that that is the level you are "supposed" to parent from. If your behavior bothers you, it is always best to work on clarifying it. Nevertheless, it is basically guaranteed that a child will not be thrilled with you and the package all the time, nor will you always enjoy your offspring's personality or behaviors.

Families are intricately bound units, bound by love, by

duty, by guilt and by many forces from the past. Children will have all sorts of overt and covert ways they control you and try to control the moving question itself. Teenagers especially are not going to be pleased about a move. Nearly always they will act mortified and martyred, feel depressed and angry, and do their best to make sure you feel guilty for forcing them into something they don't see as their choice. And, to be fair, moving is particularly wrenching at puberty. Adolescents, because they are beginning to deepen relationships, feel discomposed and emotional when ripped from newly budding friendships by a move.

What we can tell you is that because of the complex bonds you have with your children, you are unlikely to give deep consideration to a location that will ultimately not work out well for them. Your offspring will meet just the people they wanted to meet and, quite certainly, will have perfect life lessons along the way.

What this means is that when you sort through for yourself where you want to be, considering your children as much as is practical, that your choices, your heart and gut choices, are likely to work quite well for your children too—even though they may be complaining all the way. A child knows quite well, on an energetic level, where it belongs and is much more powerful in controlling what happens than you could imagine. They complain because of inconvenience and fear of the unknown, not realizing they have also chosen, on deep, energetic levels, to go where you are going.

SACRED SPOTS

As we see it, the decade of the 90s will be most mellow and enriching when spent in an area where you feel nurtured by the land, your sense of place, and the community and people. It is not necessary to get yourself situated where there are big happenings, as in Boulder or Santa Fe, or big vortices of energy as in Sedona or Mt. Shasta. Being in a location where energy is continually stirring provokes growth and change, but can be hard on the body, not restful at all. You are the one to decide which qualities you want, what is most important for you and yours at this time. Living in a location which feels right to you has everything to be said for it.

Wherever you "land", periodically you may want to make treks to the Earth's special places, the places which absorb your negative energies and cleanse your body, mind and spirit. The Earth recharges your life force most powerfully in these special power places, which may be known to you alone, or be as famous as Yosemite, as grand as Grand Canyon or as well traveled as Hawaii. It makes no difference where, as long as you allow it to alter and purify your consciousness. You know an area is sacred because of its power to move you.

Sacred spots help you awaken your innate capacity to be in an intimate, personal relationship with nature. As you open yourself, nature will reawaken your sense of wonder and give back boundless love. You might want to be open to what attracts you out of the corner of your eye, for this is the way to become tuned into nature's unseen energies. Of course, the trick is to let it remain peripheral, and not attempt to bring those energies into the center of your vision where you will immediately lose all sight and sense of them. You can't use logic or your will here; you must remain quiet and receptive. See what happens.

FENG SHUI

Once you have placed yourself—whether you have moved or not—make your space and land clear and sacred. It is fun to gather up some friends and do "house cleanings" for each other, with the idea being to get all old, rigid, stuck energy out of your house. This old stuff may belong to you or to previous dwellers in the house. This kind of purification is easiest to do in a clean house, one with cobwebs off the ceiling, dusted corners and clean windows. Old, dead energy easily clings to old, dead things.

There is no perfect way to cleanse a house since basically it is done by intention anyhow. Nevertheless, it is richer and more fun to ritualize it. Use candles, directing the fire spirits to purify your space by letting all darkness be dissolved in the golden light of the candle. Burn sage which has been bundled together and tied, letting its smoke and smell quash heavy energy in your rooms. Open your windows to push old energy out. Throw salt into the corners of rooms, and herbs like lavender or rosemary.

Be aware of which of your rooms feel clean and light after you have finished and which still feel heavy. A room may feel better except for one particular area. Often the corners of a room tend to pile up old energy and it takes extra effort to clean them. Feel your space, walk it and take charge. Keep purifying until it feels sparkly and alive to you. You can put quartz crystals with the point up in the corners of a room to energize an area which feels flat.

Also walk the perimeter of your house, creating a sense of light around it as you go. Throwing salt at the edges of the structure as you go may help you visualize this light. Feel as if your house is protected; ask for protection and love to surround your house. Get a sense of it as a special, loving place that you and loving unseen energies create together.

Also walk your land, lot or yard. Be aware of where the ground is happy and healthy and where it is not. The vegetation will offer clues. What could you do to energize the sluggish spots? What could you do to make the area more special, more sacred and more beautiful? As you put conscious energy into your land, it repays you ten fold by nurturing and supporting you.

Feng Shui is the ancient Chinese art of placing yourself in nature and housing so that the energies you receive will be beneficial and life-supporting. It is well worth investigating these eye-opening, useful concepts. As you know, the Chinese were long ago able to see how energy ran through the body (upon meridians) and see how to manipulate and balance that energy (with acupuncture) to create greater harmony and health. Feng Shui is the study of how this energy runs through nature and through man-made structures, like your house. Feng Shui also includes "fixes" for energy when it isn't sufficient or vital or harmonious.[1] In tricky times, it only makes sense to keep your environment as perfectly life-supporting as possible.

---

[1] The Sarah Rossbach books, *Feng Shui* and *Interior Design with Feng Shui,* are the best so far.

EXERCISE

This is simply a list of questions to help you get in touch with how you feel about staying put or leaving. Rate your answers, if you wish, on a scale of 1 to 10, with the low numbers meaning no, not really, not much and the high numbers meaning yes, very much. This will help you weigh your answers and see what is most important.

1. How important is it to you to feel connected with nature?   10

2. How much do you enjoy breathing the air where you now live?   10

3. In general, how committed are you to follow through once you see a change is needed.   10

4. How strong is your tendency to rethink periodically what you are doing?   10

5. If you have felt you would like to move, rate that desire or urge.   8

6. Are you annoyed with waste in your current lifestyle?   10

7. How strongly do you believe that where there is a will there is a way?   10

8. Would you like more time available for your spiritual life?   10

9. Rate your spirit of adventure.   10

10. Rate your courage.   10

11. Do you find a particular part of the country or the world "calling" to you?   10

12. How important is quiet to you? How much do you enjoy solitude?   10

13. In your present location, how *currently* important are your friends to you? (Have your connections loosened over the past year or so?)   6

14. How important is money to you?   5

15. Are you attracted to living more simply?   8

16. Rate your inclination to just float through life. 3
17. Rate your joy in being alive on an average day now. 10
18. How important is it to live close to parents or other relatives? 4
19. Rate your attachment to your current locale. 6
20. How connected to nature are you in your current location? 8
21. How much do you enjoy the ambiance of your town or city? 5
22. How involved are you? 5
22. How important do you believe it is for your children 0 to remain in the same schools and neighborhood?

CHAPTER 7

Emotional Punch
Self-Care in Dark Times

*I've had a lot of problems in my day—most of which never
happened.*
—Mark Twain

*Happiness and spiritual growth are connected. Being peaceful
and being happy form the most important foundation of spiritual practice. Then the practice goes by itself.*
—Mother Meera

STATE OF MIND VS. STATE OF PLANET

To have your personal state of mind dependent on the state
of the world is not the way to be happy—especially during the
next 20 years. If you explore and nurture your psychological and
spiritual nature, you will experience tremendous growth and transformation. In hard times, emotions tumble out more easily. Let
them roll and you will be enlivened; stifle them and you'll be depressed; do nothing but hang out with them and you'll be exhausted. It is just that simple and that difficult.

Fear will be uncoiling. Change being change, it brings panic right along with it. And what is being discussed here is not small change, but events that will require major goal and value re-evaluations from you all, as well as creative responses and reorganization from society.

FEAR & COMPANY

If you are living in Kansas and the weather is fine and life is stable, you might feel little should California suffer another devastation. "Well, that is just California and it doesn't have anything to do with me." It might as well have been one more problem in Bangladesh. Perhaps the event stirs your compassion, but unless it hits you economically, you don't feel anxious.

However, the events of the 90s are going to be so pervasive and require such major social and economic readjustments that just about everyone is likely to feel personally involved, or vulnerable, by sometime in 93. By then, people won't just be making abstract comments about June's strange cold wave, but will be concerned about the pace of change and the out-of-control feel to events. Science clearly can't stop mother nature or fix out-of-kilter weather and ecological systems—or the insects gleefully taking advantage of these new situations. Almost everybody will feel instinctive at times, Kansas included.[1]

There will be people who are loudly saying: Look, we can hold this together, don't fall into panic. Bill Clinton, like most politicians, is pragmatic, and can serve as a functional leader in these difficult times because he remains a solid, one-step-at-a-time type of thinker. Many other elected officials, local, state and national, will also rise to the occasion. Because of the responsibility of their positions, these officials will manage to process their own personal fears, or set them aside, in order to keep their part of the structure running as smoothly as possible.

---

[1] Michael uses instinctive to refer to behavior based on first chakra fears and instincts, with subsequent poor access to the reasoning intellect and to feelings of love and connection with others.

OLD SOUL EQUILIBRIUM

As a conscious soul, your job is similar: handle your fears so that you too can be helpful. Once you collect yourself, your steady vibration absolutely provides balance for others. Some of you will feel the urge and the fresh openings to take on leadership roles in your local communities.

Old souls, in particular, know that it is not useful to live with fear. Fear is not even the ideal motivation for completing a term paper. Life is life, experience is experience: it is all interesting drama. To get terribly excited or agitated throws you off center. Staying on center is important to most old souls; in fact, it is often at the cutting edge of their personal and spiritual growth. Fire walks have achieved popularity because they are a dramatic, highly graphic demonstration of the power of overcoming fear. Many of you learned that by keeping your cool you can cross hot coals without burned feet. To stay joyful and shining in times like the 90s, unless you are seriously practicing spiritual disciplines, you will need more than a little reminder here—or a fire walk experience—to remember to be detached or bemused, and to keep working through your fears.

However scattershot their approach, most old souls do explore their spiritual natures, developing unique philosophical viewpoints, personal rituals and practices. In order to remain centered, with heart and feelings open, you need to put your spiritual practices into action. In these coming times, it will definitely be important and useful to integrate your spirituality with your life.

A person who has lived many lifetimes has an advantage in rough times. Having gone through disasters, crazy karmas, food shortages and famines, political upsets, intrigues and wars gives you knowledge, breadth, and philosophical flexibility. That backlog of experience is not conscious, but it nevertheless affects your perceptions. On an essence level you know a life can get backed into a corner and then, Boom! a door opens. Suddenly you are once again swimming with options. And should no door open, you know you can survive that too—after all, here you are now. The body isn't everything. (Though when you have a body you do get attached, and rightfully so. Most people would not make it past the dangers of childhood were they not attached to their bodies and lives.)

If you become shaken because of some event, notice how awful fear feels in your body, get conscious and do some processing. Ground and calm yourself and you'll feel whole and be helpful to others again, faster than you might imagine. And process tomorrow's fears tomorrow.

The 90s present extraordinary openings for working consciously in the world. You won't want to miss these windows of opportunity by getting stuck in your own stuff. This shift will allow you to bring out your best while assisting a wavering society to move forward, and not fall backwards into a sea of chaos.

When the old approaches to life are suddenly not working, it is exciting to see what you can do in the world. New solutions are begging to be found. Most people already know many ways they would like to see the world change, be it civil rights, women's rights, animal rights, environmental rights, education, medicine, agriculture, the judicial system, taxation or television programming. Many of you will be choosing to put your time, energy, and creativity into just those areas of society that have already drawn your attention. Your unique work or life task will often be tied exactly to what you have already had (secret) dreams of changing. This is a perfect time to galvanize change, especially on local levels.

For the form of society to evolve easily, for you to get your vision happening out there in the world and for your community to remain stable, you must handle the part of you that gets scared with change—as well as the part of you that denies fear. Master your fear and you are more than free, you are a plus for everyone else.

FALLING BACK IN CONSCIOUSNESS

When panic buttons get pushed, most everyone devolves in consciousness for a while, sometimes falling right back into a primitive infant soul place, feeling scared to death, shaky and pan-icked, with no idea what to do first. Actions from this level of awareness won't often make a great deal of sense.[2] This backward fall can happen to anyone. During wars, both soldiers and civil-ians occasionally get snared into this thick level of fear, for no one has any idea what is going to happen next or how bad it will be. An ordinarily courageous person can become immobilized, or a quiet one snarly, hot-headed and dangerous.

If, when fears are provoked, a person falls back into a baby soul level of consciousness, she will comfort herself with a rigid right/wrong system of evaluations. "What's mine is mine. What happened to them, happened to them because of the sinful way they were living. Too bad, but not my problem." Acting from this consciousness, an individual finds little reason to look much past her family or small community group. Lots of judgments move right in with this level of perceiving reality. Recognizing those judgments spewing out of another person's mouth, or your own, is the best way to bring compassion back into play.

If fear slides someone into a yang, young soul place, he may grab a gun, not necessarily to shoot people but to be sure he can protect himself, his house, garden, wife, and so on. The men in an area might gather with the idea of keeping everybody else out, including those just devastated by a nearby fire or earthquake. If a person becomes fearful enough at this level of consciousness, he'll become agitated, restless, angry and feel pushed to act, though usually not in a logical or helpful way. Remind that person, or yourself, it's best to be thoughtful and act carefully in order to avoid unwanted consequences.

Falling into fear at a mature soul level of consciousness makes a person excitable, perhaps (hysterically) talkative, attentive

---

2 This is like some residents of Oakland, California, watching the firestorm on television until it was too close to think clearly about what objects and papers to pack in their cars.

to every horror story, shaky, and, in general, stuck in drama—very emotional drama. While it is healthy to acknowledge feelings, to share and cathart, when trapped at this level a person raises her degree of pain and often other people's too. Take a walk, relate to nature, pet your dog or cat, listen to an inspirational tape, do affirmations, take Rescue Remedy.[3] Do whatever it takes to get yourself calmed down.

When under stress, people often retreat into old family patterns they were imprinted with. For example, a baby soul upbringing makes it more likely a person will find herself back in that rigid, judgmental consciousness, again and again. A mature soul upbringing may have a normally calm individual yelling, gesticulating and blaming others with some regularity. When the outside world seems suddenly horrifying even the most mellow old soul is likely to slide back into an in-shock, instinctive place, for a while. Falling into any of these levels is not bad, though because they all feel so wretched, they can't be called optimal.

The advantage of having an intellectual grasp on how consciousness slides around the soul age scale is that it allows for a quick analysis. Individuals can see where they or their friends are caught and take appropriate action.

WHAT IT IS

Your sense antennas pick up a perceived threat to your well-being and suddenly you are zapped with fear and very alert. Fear makes you pay attention to what seems to be threatening you. In the body, this radar originates at the tip of your spine, in the first chakra area, but quickly its cloud can foul your entire energy field.[4] Soon, neither you nor your world looks or feels as bright.

---

[3] Bach Rescue Remedy is a homeopathic-type formulation made from flowers. Usually available at health food stores, it is immensely useful for fear states and smart to keep among the first aid supplies.

[4] Chakras are the non-physical energy vortices that act as communication links between personality and essence. There are seven main chakras, all lined up along the spine from the coccyx to the crown of your head. *Wheels of Life*, by Anodea Judith, is an excellent book about the chakra system.

Fear resonates with and ignites all the unresolved issues you carry, from this life and others. While fear always starts at the base of the spine, it may be experienced elsewhere as flutters or the tight ball in your stomach, as the heartache or heaviness in your chest, a tight or sore throat, or a blinding headache. It can make you freeze, or aggress, or run and hide.

The first chakra, or instinctive center, is a library of information dedicated to helping you preserve your body and insure physical survival. This memory bank contains permanent past-life information, often stored because of trauma, as well as present-time survival information. It contains the "Watch-out!" messages picked up from your family and culture, as well as from experiences you have perceived as being a direct threat to your existence in this lifetime.

When anything happens now which resembles, however remotely, a traumatic event from the past, your instinctive center initiates its red alert, pumping adrenalin to make you react instantaneously to the perceived threat. While the first chakra keeps you from danger, it does so by creating anxiety and panic in your body which quickens your reaction time and has, at the very least, probably helped you to avert automobile accidents. But, remembering what your body feels like after a close call will help you understand the toll these first chakra reactions take.

Living in a transforming world is both exciting and uncomfortable. Physical bodies are conservative; they like predictability. If your instinctive center is pumping adrenalin, even at low levels, for weeks at a time you'll start to feel like rubble inside. Prolonged anxiety is incredibly wearing and ultimately hurts you very much. This is one big reason why it's necessary to keep clearing fear as it comes up.

The pure vibration of fear is leaden—no light, no hope, no fun, somber, dense and very limiting. Fear makes you feel small and insecure. How could it not drag you down? And then, adding insult to injury, it will bring up the progeny you'd rather ignore—those shoved-under-the-rug, but still pesky bottom-line issues such as fear of abandonment and loneliness, or feelings of powerlessness and vulnerability, fear of failure, fear of rejection and even fear of self-expression. So the good news is that as the events of the decade confront you, you will also be clearing away your underlying issues, processing the old personal stuff you have carried around for decades—or lifetimes.

GETTING THE MESSAGE

If you don't release fear you paralyze your life energy. How to let go? The first action we suggest is give this instinctive center message some respect. Thank it for warning you, for showing you something that you need to beware of. Ultimately, you want neither to resist nor dwell on these fear messages, but rather to acknowledge their value. Aim to interpret this communication as clearly as you can. Study the message. Don't just force away the negativity—or give in. And don't bottle it up either; that is asking for sickness. You want to see the truth and reality of a situation so you can deal with it optimally. Then you are empowered.

Should you be having trouble getting the message, you might want to do a short visualization. Put yourself into a relaxed, meditative state. Pull your inquisitive psychic energy inward, let go of the world. Listen to a relaxation or meditation tape if you need support in letting go of the jangles and to obtain a relaxed state.

Become aware of your instinctive center, that energetic ball of energy at the base of your spine. Acknowledge it and then, in your imagination, bring that ball up to the level of your mind so that you can take a look at it to see what is there. You will become aware of a feeling or image, perhaps you will hear words. Stay with what is happening for a minute or so and see where it leads into your life now.

Quickly write down what happened before it becomes obscure. Getting and keeping first chakra information conscious is often tricky in the extreme. It may be easier to work with a friend who can lead you through the process, keep asking questions and keep you focused. You may feel like you made everything up or that you didn't see enough to be of help. Looking at these stored first chakra patterns and messages is almost always difficult. After all, this thick old sludge pool of stuff is not physical; neither is it right here, right now. On top of that, the instinctive center tends to feel taboo, like an energetic hot potato. What it stores are not your proudest moments or highest thoughts. This area is not fun like hanging out at your seventh chakra all close to God, the angels and your higher self can be. However, on your road to wholeness, it is necessary to make friends with your first chakra. It is inescapable.

FINDING THE LIE AND THE TRUTH

The next step in releasing fear is to find the lie. Perhaps the message is that you are boxed in by circumstances and will never be able to get out, that your life will keep spinning in unproductive circles. The truth may be that you are scrunched by circumstance now, but it is not a dangerous situation in and of itself. It simply resonates with old fears that you carry from the many times you have been boxed in by life and either couldn't get out, or gave up.

Or, perhaps the fear is that you won't be able to put food on the table for your children. The truth may be that even though economic and environmental conditions are worsening, you can still provide the basics. You can grow food if need be and request help and protection from the devic world.[5] Furthermore, this is not the 13th Century; you are not a hapless peasant whose children must beg and steal. Release your urgency.

The next step is to declare for yourself what is true. Better than a negative such as, "I am not in any danger now," is a powerful affirmative statement, one which you would dearly love to be true. How about, "I handle life's changes beautifully." or, "I

[5] See any of the various books about the Findhorn gardens or Machaelle Wright's books on her Perelandra gardens.

trust life and grow from my challenges." Affirmations are short, positive statements which make you feel good and motivate you to get back on track. While you are in the process of change, your mind can cling to affirmations instead of going wild and fearful. Writing affirmations 20 or 30 times until you begin to feel at cause, not at effect, is powerful. You can feel the shift in your body.[6]

LETTING GO

The last step is to let go. Give that first chakra a sense of relief. Remind yourself you can release that quaking, uncomfortable energy, instead of doing the "normal" thing, clutching tightly to it. Letting go means opening the chakra and allowing it to drain. This feels a bit like relaxing this area and letting excess energy fall down towards the center of the earth where it can be healed.[7]

It is quite ethical to permit this negative, fear energy of yours to drain into the earth. The earth may be burdened to a breaking point by physical pollution with ecosystems no longer able to clean and renew themselves, but it is wholly capable of re-cycling psychological energy, negative as you want to make it. When you have a body you are inextricably linked with the earth and can look to it for support.

GROUNDING

The final part of the fear releasing process is to imagine a small cord with an anchor on it dropping down from your first chakra and being magnetized towards the center of the earth. At the core of the earth, imagine hooking this line onto rocks or energy grids, whatever you feel is there. For healing purposes, it is best to visualize the center of the earth as cool, safe, caring and very stable (as opposed to molten red and devilish). You might like to vi-

---

6 *You Can Heal Your Life* by Louise Hay and *The Dynamic Laws of Healing* by Catherine Ponder are two books which deal with recognizing and changing limited thinking. Both are full of suggested affirmations.

7 See exercise at the end of this chapter.

sualize the center of the earth as Goddess energy, powerful, good, giving, and as softly radiant as pearls. It is High Being energy, like Christ, or Buddha or Krishna, but slightly different because it comes from within the planet. This is what you want to relate to. With this anchoring cord pulled taut, you feel more secure; also excess or negative energies can travel down the cord to the earth's center.

When you are first creating a grounding cord, it is likely to feel cumbersome, and silly; hard to visualize or feel, much less keep in place. But as you work with it, the whole process becomes easier and will start to feel very right. When you have a body, which is now, keeping that cord there all the time is a highly useful habit to acquire, with payoffs that are worth your trouble.

An anchoring cord is actually a normal part of the healthy body's energy patterns; it is a natural occurrence, usually quite unconscious. But this energetic connection to the planet is something that tends to disappear when a culture gets overly intellectual, like the U.S., Japan or Northern Europe. Then, you must consciously connect. Being grounded helps keep your body healthy, it helps you relate to nature and maintain a sense of security in the world. Grounding helps keep your head out of the ozone and you out of trouble. Plus, by pulling earth energy up into your body, you help yourself manifest the physical things that you want.

Is it going to be harder to root down into the earth when the earth feels untrustworthy? You bet! At those points in time, it is useful to imagine some protection around your cord so that you don't soak up the uneasiness present in the earth's crust. The core, which is not affected by what is going on at the surface, will always feel stable; the axis could shift 15 degrees and the core is still going to be secure, nurturing and comfortable.

Should you care to do some earth healing, send loving vibrations to the earth through the cord. When the earth feels uneasy, this is a wonderful thing to do. Instead of sucking in uncomfortable vibrations, you send out peace, love and stability. Hardly anything is more unnerving than to feel the earth is out of control and that it may not support you. It is one thing to have to deal with a madman, or a dangerous part of a city, but when the earth is suddenly not dependable you wonder what is. Sending love out to the earth through your grounding cord will help you get beyond fear and be rebalanced more quickly.

GAIA AND GOD

Earth is an unusually beautiful planet. The purity of nature, undisturbed and natural, is stunning. The spirit of the earth, which is increasingly being referred to as Gaia, is easy to experience during your tuned-in moments. Gaia is the pretty surface of the planet you all enjoy, but also the heart of the earth. Tapping into nature's largess, into Gaia, is one of the wonderful things that happens more spontaneously with a grounding cord. Having this conscious sense of connection can lead towards greater inner peace.

Linking through the crown chakra[8] with the Tao, your guides and higher self is something most old souls occasionally experiment with. These upper chakras are fun to play with and experience. However, the difficulty for older souls is that typically the upper chakras are too open and active to be in balance with the lower ones which are often ignored, sometimes to the degree that earning a decent living becomes difficult.

It is every bit as important to be connected to the heart of the planet, the earth, as it is to be connected to the heavens. Because access to the earth is gained through the lower chakras, which seem icky, this link is often lost. As humans are more powerful and happy when relating to both body and spirit, conscious lifelines down into the earth as well as up to the Tao are recommended. Especially in difficult times, it is worth the effort to heal your instinctive center and get in good relationship with it and the earth.

---

8   The energetic center at the top of the head.

NOT 'TILL DEATH DO US PART

We offer you another inducement for making friends with your instinctive center. It always stays with you; all its unresolved issues remain with you, occasionally acting up, until you handle them in this or future lifetimes. When you die, your emotional, intellectual and moving centers die right along with the body. But, all that your life has been is stored in the instinctive center as a pattern of energy and goes with you. Where essence goes, the instinctive center goes: as essence pulls the instinctive center out of the body at death, the body will then weigh almost an ounce less. Your essence will plug it into the next body like a tape cassette into a tape recorder. It will carry on with all the issues and fears you've accumulated until you heal and release them.

PITH AND MARROW?

Fear is a challenge. Know that some heroism is being called for, maybe big, maybe not, but we think it heroic to keep dropping fear and moving towards positive action. You will be developing courage and discipline as you continue to handle your apprehensions.

Dropping your fears for even one moment is better than never getting separate from fear. It is akin to stopping the mind for even a few seconds as you meditate. Benefits accrue from even those small beginning moments of peace. Clearing fear from the body is almost as much an ongoing process as clearing chatter from the mind.

Dealing consciously with inner issues as they arise allow parents to be stabilizing factors for their children, which then allows the children to be stabilizing to their friends and in their school situations. A balanced or happy person has a ripple effect that allows others to relax their own first chakras and fear issues. Conversely, one person's anxiety can ignite the first chakra reflexes of many; suddenly everybody is off and running. First chakras are genius at picking up when someone is in fear, whether that person is consciously aware or denying any problem. Fearful people affect others greatly by vibrations alone, but so do balanced, loving old souls.

SADNESS

When the earth is unsteady, your whole life can feel insecure. Sadness creeps in to the body and personality when your hopes are dashed and expectations unfulfilled. It makes you droop and stoop and whine. Sadness is a sign you are attached to life being one way, your way. You need to let go.

Sadness will be a basic response to the surprises and blows of the next twenty years. Sadness comes on because of grief that you can't have it your way, that you can't control the world. If you go through it, you clear the air and melt the rigidity that says life must be on your own terms. Cry, sing the blues, regret life, let loose, complain, wail and wallow. Enjoy it and the sadness will let you go. Avoid it, suppress it, and you'll go gray and depressed. As you move through sadness, fear and anger, you come out lighter, clearer and stronger than before.

SELF-CARE IN DARK TIMES

Here are yet more ways to nurture, lift and center yourself. Sitting in front of a fire is peaceful and comforting. The element of (contained) fire is exceedingly soothing to the first chakra and to a body having survival worries. Fire is like a doorway which connects you with all that is ancient on the planet. Red wine or home brew can give succor and nourish too, as can friends, of course, and your companion animals. Sing, chant, dance and make music; all are healing. Invite your friends and build some wonderful fires and evenings.

Bring out your humor or put yourself in the vicinity of those who make you laugh. Value those who can disengage from misery long enough to find the funny side of life. Comic relief is always healing, and oftentimes it gives needed perspective.

Food can make you feel secure and comforted. However if you overdose, you go unconscious and back to the discomfort of square one. It is smart to be aware of your own comfort foods and use them as consciously as you can. Some people drown themselves in pizza, others immediately head for sweets; creamy childhood memories pull others towards ice cream, macaroni and cheese, or mashed potatoes and gravy. Be mindful. Getting comfort from food can present problems—or comfort from alcohol or any other drug, legal or not. You've got to do your processing, your inner work, and you can't do it in oblivion. So use food and drugs with care. In fact, eating well and cleanly will bring you to balance and strength most easily. Walking, cycling, jogging, dancing, yoga, tai chi and aikido all help maintain healthy balance in your body and mind.

Wake up early and greet the new sun. Find a good viewing spot and watch the sunset. Walk a scenic path. Bask in light of the full moon. Take time to smell the flowers, the grass, and the air. Go to the park and use the swings. Take a bath by candlelight. Burn rose incense. Ask a special friend to read to you. There are many, many ways to nurture yourself, but you have to make them happen. Find a balance in your giving and receiving.

EATING FOR HEALTH

Bodies are very different from each other, unique in what they need and in what they don't process well. Because these times are emotional and because of assaults from ultraviolet radiation, two well-known immune system downers, we think it important to mention a few things about food.

Number one: preparing and eating your food, whatever it is, with love and gratefulness transforms that food so that it is more agreeable to your body and more supportive of it.

Number two: for a large majority of people, the healthiest way to eat is non-fanatic macrobiotic, (which, unfortunately, is nearly a contradiction in terms).[9] It means eating primarily whole grains, like brown rice, barley and millet, beans and cooked vegetables, and small slivers of animal proteins. Liquids are taken in small amounts. The finishing touches are sea vegetables (seaweeds) and fermented or cultured products like true soy sauce, miso, sauerkraut and so on. Macrobiotics tends to exclude most fruits and all dairy products. A diet like this puts no strain on your body, gets rid of cravings fairly quickly, helps you maintain balance and calm, and it keeps your body strong and its defenses alert. If you are having trouble fending off illnesses, you might try eating along these lines.

Periodic cleanses are also helpful. Existing for a few days on dilute fruit juices or an alkaline vegetable broth or a miso broth, resting, and using a psyllium seed preparation to keep your bowels moving will go a long way toward getting toxic debris out of your body and maintaining a high degree of health.[10]

NATURE'S HELPERS

Gemstones and minerals are part of nature's bounteous gift to humans. All exert a positive, beneficial effect on a person in contact with them. Appropriate stones can make life flow more easily. You can grow faster and more comfortably under their influence.

For better or worse, your environment always affects you. Rocks and gemstones are particularly potent parts of the human environment. Stones can help you maintain balance in your life and assist you to work effectively on the parts of your personality or life that cause you trouble. The strongest effect usually comes from wearing stones, either on the skin or in a pocket. You don't need to be particular over which chakra or on what finger you place these stones. They will fill your energy field with their ener-

---

9 Michio Kushi is the most well-known proponent of this manner of eating and healing. He has written many books including *The Macrobiotic Book*.

10 Check with your health professional first.

gy, regardless of their starting point. Placing larger minerals in a room gradually fills up the room with the stones' energies, thus contributing those vibrations to people using the room.

What follows are some generally easy-to-find minerals which are advantageous in difficult times.[11] Choose the ones you are attracted to, always opting for the stone which most draws you. Sometimes it's the dazzling green one, and sometimes the plain mottled brown one.

Freezing any stone, once a week or so, will help keep it energetically fresh. Overnight in the freezer usually does it. The process doesn't disturb your food. The stone contracts with the cold and then lets go of any exogenous energy it may have picked up as it defrosts. Soaking stones in sea salt and water baths in the sun and moonlight is renewing and a good way to pamper your stones occasionally. A stone which is in your ring or pocket is a thousand times more likely to become drained, clogged or exhausted than a stone left in its natural setting. So, give your helpers a break and keep them energetically clean.

GEMSTONES

Shells of all kinds, including mother of pearl and abalone, plus bone, ivory, flint and petrified wood are the basic calmers of anxiety, worry, and survival fears. They are grounding, and tend to make a person feel everything will work out in the long run.

Rose quartz assists a person in staying aligned with his essence. For those among you who tend to float off, this stone will help keep your essence in your body and your feet on the ground. It helps heal your heart too.

Leopardskin agate, which is usually easy to find, is strong in effect, very calming, healing and helpful for dealing with heavy, deep emotional impacts. Black coral is also a major healer of anxiety and survival-oriented fears. It can help you to see your issues clearly so that you are able to handle them with more ease.

---

[11] For a very complete listing consult, *Michael's Gemstone Dictionary*, David and Van Hulle. This is an excellent resource book.

Blue aventurine keeps the first chakra, and the feet, open and unblocked so energy can flow through unimpeded. Red calcite allows negative emotions to drain more easily from the body. Moonstone inspires you and gives the feeling that anything is possible.

Green jade, well-loved in Asia where lives tend to be tougher, creates a mood of tranquility and helps the wearer emanate a calm peacefulness. Gray and brown jades both drain excess energy from all chakras which allows them to re-balance. This is especially useful when you are feeling jammed up, stressed and confused.

The lace agates, blue, white and lavender, all create the secure, strong feeling that as new situations arise they can be handled. Even very stubborn people are helped to be more flexible and encouraged and assured that life won't collapse into something overwhelming.

Pearls, sugilite, malachite and granite all balance all the chakras. Pearls have the virtue of enhancing wisdom. Sugilite facilitates receptivity to higher wisdom and is an excellent channeling stone. Malachite increases loving tolerance and a beautiful, balanced feeling in the body. Granite paves the way to a direct connection with heaven and earth because its supportive of the first chakra and the seventh.

Gemstones and minerals can't do your work for you, but they are tools which help you grow in the directions you choose. In a body, it only makes sense to take advantage of these benign helpers that give so easily and freely of their energies.

MORE GROUNDING

You ground yourself energetically by visualizing a cord which roots you into the Earth. This was discussed at some length already because it is not common knowledge, and it is vital. It is also important to ground yourself physically, psychologically and spiritually.

You ground yourself physically by taking care of your body

and health. You exercise, eat well and groom yourself. You also ground yourself physically by taking care of your space, keeping it orderly and clean, and by keeping your plants and animals happy and healthy.

You gain psychological grounding by your commitment to grow, through your dedication to cleaning out your fears, angers, past hurts, sad stories and unhappiness. You also gain psychological grounding by prioritizing so that all parts of your life get attention and time. Life has a richer texture when work, play, service, time alone, relationships, movies and metaphysics are balanced.

Spiritual grounding comes from slowing down enough to touch that which is absolute. You get it many places: from reiki, yoga or tai chi; from reading spiritual and metaphysical books; from meditation or church or pagan ceremonies. What matters is that you personally take the time to find the forms that enable you to touch in with what is absolute and timeless.

Years like these will push you to transform yourself; otherwise, you suffer relentlessly. You will do best by staying calm and releasing urgency; by noticing and letting go of attachments (stocks, weather, life-style); by turning inward and upward to keep your vision and overview clear; and by making yourself useful in your community.

EARTH MEDITATION

This is a grounding exercise, optimally for daily use until you feel yourself to be grounded most of the time. For most people, this won't come until you have practiced for a month or so. We are presuming that most of you know how to get quiet, relax your breathing and give yourself the time and space to alter your consciousness slightly.

To do this exercise, you can either lie or sit. If you are sitting, it is helpful to have your back fairly straight. Since this exercise is lengthy, it will probably work best to record it for yourself, reading the words into your machine while you are in a slightly altered state. Then, you have it to play back whenever you want.

First of all take a few slow breaths through your nose to relax yourself. Enjoy the exhalations, breathing out softly through your mouth. Breathe slowly, begin to feel yourself relaxing. Let your body start to get heavy; feel your weight in the chair or against the floor.

Now, become aware of the top of your head. Open your crown chakra by allowing the area to relax. The top of your head may feel warm as you relax and open. You may see light there, shimmering white, or silver and gold. Keep breathing. Allow yourself to feel the connection to your higher self, to your soul. Ask your soul to make the connection stronger. Feel the love. Bask in it.

Now, move your consciousness to your first chakra at the base of your spine. Take a few breaths while being aware of that first chakra and still keeping your crown chakra open. Breathe in. Feel like you are breathing in through the first chakra. When you exhale, feel your breath going right through the first chakra area and stimulating this red ball of energy. Breathe in through the chakra, hold the exhalation momentarily and then breathe out through the chakra. Do this several times. Soon you will be able to feel the vortex of energy there. As you breathe into any chakra, its energy becomes more coherent and vital.

Keeping your consciousness on the first chakra, imagine drop-

ping a little cord from it towards the center of the Earth. This cord is going to anchor you to the Earth's nurturing energy. Keep your chakra loose and relaxed as you let the cord sink into the center of the Earth. Let your cord quickly be pulled towards the center of the Earth. You are now vitally connected with your planet. If the cord you sent down is narrow, like the size of a pencil, experiment by expanding it to the diameter of a garden hose. See what that does to the energy. Again, secure it tightly into the center of the Earth. Be aware of the magnetism between your first chakra and the center of the Earth.

Now, if you wish to let go of all that is negative, undesired or unhealthy in your body, imagine a giant vacuum in the center of the Earth. Turn on the switch and let it clean you by pulling all that is negative or old from you. Take a few deep breaths while this is happening. Keep your first chakra area open; keep yourself relaxed. Let all that is negative and uncomfortable be released to the center of the Earth. Thank the Earth, acknowledge it. Ask your higher self to place light into those newly empty areas of your body. Breathe in the light and let it circulate, glow and be absorbed by your body.

If you wish at this time to journey to the center of the Earth, again place your consciousness at your first chakra. Now start moving your consciousness slowly down that cord through the Earth, through dirt, through rocks, through water, into caves of rose quartz and amethyst—slide through all of that, following your cord into the center of your planet.

Be aware of how deep you feel, how peaceful—let yourself be nurtured by the Earth. Ask it to nurture you, to give you love, to feed you love. Keep breathing, take a minute or two to really enjoy the nurturing you are receiving. The center of the Earth always feels peaceful and good, it is always calm and nurturing. You can renew your spirit here and your body. This energy is very good for your body. When you are ready, bring your consciousness back up your cord, through the Earth, back into your body.

Notice your cord and make sure it is still well connected to the

Earth's center. You can then swim, jog, ride in cars, motorcycles or airplanes and still have your grounding cord connected. In fact, you will always be safer for it. If your cord is not pulled tight, pull it tight now. Notice how that feels. Give your cord a color. Use earthy colors, not white. Make it shimmer, make it alive, but keep it earthy brown or green or orange, red or ocher to keep your body happy and well-nourished.

If you wish, bring this light up into your abdomen. Fill your abdomen with this light. Now, bring the light up to your third chakra at your navel and then up to your heart chakra at mid-chest level. Bring that Earth energy up to your heart and let it stream out—direct it to all the people that you love, to your house, your projects, the people in your town and the world. It is a beautiful energy. Let more come into your body and stream out your heart. Run that Earth energy through. This is a very healing energy, and quite different from what comes in through the crown of your head.

Now be aware of your crown chakra. Allow it to gently open while you keep your first chakra open also; let your entire spine be filled with the light streaming in from above and below, from both these chakras. Let these energies blend in your heart. Feel yourself magnificent, glowing with light. Ask for inspiration, for clarity, for healing, for all you want. If you would like to sit and bask in this energy, take some time now.

When you are ready to come back to your day and your life, thank all your helpers. Ask that your chakras be balanced and made appropriate for daily life. Your energy has been very far out in the universe; draw it all back to you. Draw your energy to you from in front of you, behind you, above and below you. You are refreshed, back in your body and ready for life. Enjoy your wonderful day.

CHAPTER 8

Off the Beaten Track
Men and Women

A not so modest proposal for safer streets:
What this country needs is a federal law forbidding men to go
out on the streets unless they are accompanied by a woman.
—Judy MacLean

It is now possible for a flight attendant to get a pilot pregnant.
—Richard Ferris, President, United Airlines

POWER BATTLE

In the young soul power battle between the sexes, men won. That doesn't mean they won every skirmish, or found peace at home, but they held life's stronger cards. The quality and scope of most lifetimes depended greatly on the sex of the body you chose. You received very different types of experience with each sex, adding to your development and to the richness and complexity of your human résumé. In a male body you were virtually guaranteed not only more muscle but also more privilege, both of which counted abundantly in a young soul world. Thus power, the quintessential young soul pleasure, was easier to obtain with a male body due both to its greater size and strength and to the way most societies were structured.

It only figures that a young soul world would spark inequality between the sexes. One sex was bound to gain authority over the other. And in fact, men and women have been out of harmony since Greek times—robustly out of harmony since the Roman era. The epochs before that saw cultures which honored men and women equally, and others in which either men or women prevailed. The pendulum on earth has swung back and forth between male and female domination, with shorter periods of peace and equality at the end zones of one sex's domination of the other. When the earth grows into its old soul phase, men and women will gradually give up their power struggles with each other. At minimum, that is one thousand years from now.[1]

IMPULSIVE AND IMPASSIONED

Mature souls will create male and female interactions expressive of mature soul dynamics. Men and women will be looking at each other with more interest, desire, emotional intensity and sexual longing, while simultaneously yearning for peace and balance. Mature souls value stable family life, yet they want to feel alive, vital and challenged to grow. Sounds confusing, right? Add to that the tug-of-war women will feel between their thirst to take advantage of powerful new opportunities in the world and the mature soul hunger for high romance.

The thrust of the 90s creates a flourishing climate for male-female intimacy. With so many economic, environmental and spiritual challenges, men and women are pushed into handling the outside world rather than concentrating on personal conflicts. When focused on problematic events, couples tend to pull together, forget surface irritations and bond ever more deeply as they handle outer issues.

---

[1] As a planet gets into the late stages of development and begins to be dominated by mature and old souls, life always speeds up, growth time is compressed, and everyone is pulled forward more quickly. That is why the baby soul era took three to four times as long as the young soul era, and why the young soul era took three or four times as long as the mature soul era will.

Individuals develop inner strength in hard times; couples often develop a deep, abiding trust in each other. Normal mature soul dramatics—petty bickering, simmering jealousies, bouts of insecurity, affairs born of boredom—are suddenly relegated to the back burner. When enough of these difficult events are set in motion, your own soap opera will seem extraneous.

As people move into their heart centers and away from their power centers, the desire for vital relationships will be strong. Given the new consciousness climate, fewer men will be blind to women's issues—mature soul men are more likely to be concerned with making life fair for everyone than in sticking to their advantages. As men pull back from domination, they leave more room for a relational and emotional life. Societal support for the emotional evolvement of men will be strong—you can already see that occurring. The value of women will soon move up another notch simply because the average female is much more knowledgeable about the emotional, intuitive world than the average male. Basically because of the way the two sexes are influenced by hormones, women will continue to have easier expertise in the inner world and men easier expertise in the outer.

Boundaries between the sexes are breaking down and will continue to do so over the next two decades. Those 50 and 60 year olds with heavily fortified opinions about what is appropriate behavior for a woman or a man are already increasingly being seen as old-fashioned, out-of-touch. Parents who try to imprint their children with locked-in, constricted sexual stereotypes will have a tough time because neither society nor the media will support them. In most Western societies, younger people who attempt to live from narrowly defined sex roles will be viewed as inept and stunted by their peers. In the near future, there will be few legal or social partitions between what a woman can do and what a man can do. Baby souls don't change easily, so many will cling ferociously to the old ways of doing things, but they are being propelled along by change like everybody else.

Mature soul energetics have already supported men to open their hearts and feeling natures, allowing them to be more tender fathers and kinder participants in life. Some men, to the humankind's surprise, found they exulted in staying home and not being out there in the world with traditional male occupations. In the last decade, Western men have made tremendous leaps toward knowing themselves; they have been identifying and expressing feelings and integrating their active, intellectual sides with their inner perceptivity. Men will continue to unchain themselves from the flat, one-sided productivity society seemed to demand of them.

Much of this current male growth was predicated on women stepping into their own power. In finding their voices, women allowed men to soften; men lost their excuse, or their need, to be strong all the time. While men were originally very uneasy, very much threatened by the fortitude with which women were insisting on power, by now many are adjusted, able to enjoy the advantages of the new situation. The younger the man and the older the soul, the easier the adjustment tended to be.

WARRIOR WOMEN

How did it happen that the lot of women changed so quickly? It relates to good astral planning and fortunate political timing. Pushing the female sex ahead looked like an interesting task; a process which would turn lives upside down and give variety to the man-woman experience. And, it was time for the pendulum to swing.

Starting early in the century, handfuls of interested souls (the shock troops) put themselves in female bodies on the front lines, determinedly pushing to make women and society aware of the severe limitations placed on their sex. Laws changed and thinking began to change, but it wasn't until the 70s that the critical mass necessary to make major societal shifts was incarnate and stirring. Large numbers of women in their teens, twenties and thirties were suddenly unwilling to put up with the same old lives or lies. They started to stand up for themselves, and were willing to punch the guys, or the system, in the nose when handed can't-do lines. This can-do mass of young, mature and old soul women managed to get their feet in new doors, creating myriad new openings for their sex's fuller participation in life.

Many, many, of these women were warriors, the role that is feisty, strong of body and most inclined to fight for principles.[2] Warriors often tend to choose and savor the physicality of male lifetimes—and suddenly here they were, women with agendas. Traditionally the U.S. has had almost 30% warriors, mostly male. This was very good for business and for keeping the country running in an organized fashion. With a very high proportion of these warriors being born women over the last few decades, you can see that this role became a very significant part—nearly half—of the under-35 female population.

Putting sturdy warrior women on the front lines was good tactical thinking on the part of the astral committees planning this historical change—and it worked. (Astral plans don't always manifest perfectly. All the mature and old souls who excitedly incarnated into Russia in the 30s and 40s in order to create an equitable society weren't so lucky; most of them ended up with severely restricted lifetimes.) But these contemporary warrior women are doing fine, gaining more power every year while redefining the way society thinks a woman should look (more muscles), act and think (more independent).

In the next twenty years, opportunities for women will continue to enlarge. Girls born in the 80s and 90s will barely realize how major were the changes or how difficult the struggle that made the openings they step through as a normal part of existence. Boys won't be any more aware of how much the world changed to

2 Michael's systematic way of looking at the universe identifies seven "roles", warrior being one. Whatever role you are, you keep it in every life, getting good and comfortable with it. Each role has favorite kinds of behavior and a particular manner in which it gives to all the other roles. Warriors are organized types who enjoy the challenges and pleasures of the physical plane. See my *The World According to Michael* or other Michael books listed at the back of this book for complete explanations.

allow for the fuller expression of their feeling natures. When flowing right along with a major consciousness change, what is new becomes normal with amazing speed.

It is difficult for a first-world person from a Western country to comprehend that at this current juncture only small pockets of humanity believe women are equal beings. Many, many more still see women as a kind of sub-species, property with no rights. But, with the exception of isolated enclaves of more traditional peoples, it won't be too much longer before most cultures on the planet come to the realization that women are in fact human and have rights, possibly even equal rights, to the pleasures and responsibilities of the world. For the majority of the earth's population, that is only a suspect notion—like the idea circulating among dolphins and whales that humans may be sentient, ensouled beings, and not simply dangerous, unthinking primitives.

However, as we've mentioned, this mature soul consciousness shift is strong and compelling. The manner in which the powerful Western world "allows" its women to act—in and out of films—starts to affect men, women and cultures worldwide. Madonna's anti-patriarchal message is coming in loud and clear. On the other hand, it will be a while before Rambo takes a dive at the third world box office.

The surge toward fundamentalism in the Middle East, by men and women, is in part a reaction against making changes in the way women are viewed and treated, but some of this recalcitrance comes from essence level needs to keep these old male-female dichotomies available for experience now—and to keep the drama open for future lifetimes too.

GOD THE FATHER STEPS DOWN

As long as a patriarchal religion is the spiritual viewpoint of choice, inequality between the sexes will persist. In people's minds, God being one sex makes the other sex lower. Though some Christian churches are expanding the role of women and their viewpoint toward them, not one has added Goddess worship. It is rare for established religions to recast themselves and lead people forward; few are free to change with evolving societal needs. Worldwide, religions are very much stuck. People have a need for new institutions as well as new spiritual leaders.

About twenty-five years from now, we see it likely that four or five infinite souls will make an appearance and, as they are prone to do, greatly change the world.[3] These great and loving beings will be both male and female and their skin colors will embrace different corners of the world. All will have essentially the same message—love each other, respect each other, honor nature. These luminous souls will very greatly affect the way religion is practiced, making it more nature oriented and less patriarchal. Having two or three female infinite souls of varying races will give a fantastic lift to the way everyone views women and take women's lives to yet another level.

NEW TO POWER?

When any group has been kept from power for a long period and then gains some, it is prone to acting up. A lot of the nastiness women were engaging in in the 70s (as well as the current infighting among blacks in South Africa and ethnic groups in the old Soviet bloc) is the result of being disenfranchised for such a long time. You act like an adolescent for a while, work it out and come to a new level of maturity and responsibility. Change is always roughest when first launched. Sometimes it is necessary to be noisy, cranky and disobedient to demand attention. Nevertheless, the mature soul will begin to see clearly that people are one—at that point the necessity of finding compassion and getting along

---

3 Each infinite soul, although residing in one body, is actually a group of souls so large and all-encompassing that it is just a breath away from the Tao, from All-That-Is; or, in other words, from God. Infinite souls are always very affecting, and come typically in times of great change and need. The most recent infinite souls have been Christ, Buddha, Lao Tse, Krishna and Quetzalcoatl, all of whom helped smooth the world's transition into young soul consciousness. There have previously been many infinite souls in female bodies, whose names now linger as old Goddess names like Astarte and Bridget.

becomes obvious. People will begin to view others, including the opposite sex, as interesting variations of the human fabric, as opposed to the us-versus-them consciousness of the young soul.

WHO'S GOT THE RULES?

As parity between the sexes increases, customary patterns of behavior fall into meaninglessness. For this reason, mature soul times can get very disarrayed. How is it all supposed to be? Who's on first? What's a homer, anyhow? Ruts, grooves and self-evident truths can't hold you in place, and new truths have little chance of turning into reliable dogma because everything changes too often. That's part of the fun—and a good part of the trouble.

The average person on the planet has now had dozens of past lives and many female and male bodies. Even without conscious recall, this extensive backlog of experience with each body affects a person's thinking. A mature or old soul is innately less comfortable with sexism (or racism), be he or she American or Saudi, though how you were raised and imprinted always takes some getting over. Eventually it starts to seem crazy to limit what anybody can do or feel by the type of genitals (or skin) possessed. This larger backlog of past life experience is one more nail in the thinking that limits the behavior, achievements and status of women (or people of color).

If you have lived but ten or 20 lifetimes, you are going to remain strongly identified with your body and your society of the moment. But when like most beginning mature souls you have lived 80 to 120 lifetimes, that identification gradually loosens and lightens. A part of you knows that you are not your body, that social rules always change, and that a person can be quite feminine, yet competently run a business, or be strongly male, and cry, dance and nurture others. In mature soul times, the rules of appropriate behavior get pretty marshy: this makes for conflict, high emotional intensity, as well as occasional backlashes from segments of society that want clear definitions and limits, not bounding change. Antiabortion rabidity and other combat against women's rights will be around for awhile, keeping life between the sexes—and the soul ages—quite spicy.

YET MORE SPICE

Another factor making life ever more interesting between the sexes is the fact that many people are in the body they enjoy less, choose less often and thus have less experience with. In your early lifetimes, you tend to take on more lifetimes in the body which feels more comfortable to you. By the time mature soul lifetimes come around, your essence begins to exert a mild pressure to get experience balanced. Old souls are under stronger essence pressure to balance out their male and female experiences, essentially because it becomes now or never. As the world begins to have large numbers of mature and old souls, it is more common to find people who have enjoyed the independence, strength and power of male bodies experimenting with women's bodies and, of course, paying back karmas they instigated in their male lifetimes. Essences who have enjoyed the connectedness, creativity and pro-creativity of female lifetimes will now be balancing themselves by taking on male experience and karmas.

It makes an interesting soup: women who are more used to being men and men who are more experienced being women. You can see the results of this everywhere in North America and Europe. This recipe for confusion has already helped loosen the confined ways female and male were previously expected to act. Madonna and Michael Jackson are strong, unique examples of what we are speaking of here. While they are each experiencing and learning from bodies somewhat foreign to them, they have become role models, perhaps we should say model breakers, for many young people. Most of the girls who idolize Madonna won't have her talent or acute instincts, but her outrageous strength is impressed on their minds forever. She is a nervy, masterful heroine unlikely to trip herself up as she takes on the patriarchy. Michael

Jackson, a more virginal type than Madonna, is not someone boys are likely to directly emulate, but he is out there living a soft, poetic, rather magical existence and getting away with it.

Typically, but by no means universally, it is the softer, sensitive male who has had more experience with female lifetimes and the tougher, more determined female who has taken on more male lifetimes. As all this continues to be mixed on a greater-than-before scale, evolution towards a more equal, more blended, male and female quickens. In the meantime, it can be highly disorienting for all participants, for there are no clear guideposts and little steady ground. Every time you think you have your bearings, the sands shift again.

In the West, the most tumultuous part of this process is already complete. Nobody much expects the sexes to be like the men and women of the 40s, or even the 60s. The warrior women have done their job; Western society let go of a goodly amount of its sexist shoulds and musts—and no longer clings tenaciously to what is left. The tone is set for the rest of the world—when it decides to follow along.

HORMONAL WASHES

On planet Earth, the innate singularity of each sex is stronger than on 95% of all other planets where sentient, conscious life exists. Earth is an experimental planet, and one of the biggest experiments humans are engaged in is having many of the most powerful and interesting karmas take place between the sexes. It is not easy for humans to understand how unusually wide the differences between men and women are since it is all you have known. These differences make for disparate approaches to life—and easy misunderstandings, intense and powerful karmas. Cetaceans, the other sentient, conscious species on earth, exemplify the more universal androgynous, undifferentiated look and feel of male and female. As mammals they have role demarcations, but cetaceans do not have the strong male-female emotional karmas which so color human life. (Their karmas are centered around strong, compelling needs to innovatively and beautifully express themselves, and their understanding of life.)

Before we go further, it would be useful to mention that even though the demarcations between what women and men can *do* are getting erased, their body energies are always going to be quite distinct from each other. The hormones which infiltrate the two bodies are pervasive and highly influential and create markedly different fields in which behavior takes place.

The unique hormonal wash each body gets lasts for about 40 years each lifetime. Until hormones begin to swarm at approximately age twelve, children are in what we call an innocent phase; after age 52 or so hormones calm down, thereby enabling each sex to enter what we call the wisdom phase, a centered, reflective period of life no longer unsettled by hormones pushing the body and emotions this way and that.

FEMALE BODIES

For obvious reasons, women's hormonal cycles are easier to identify and get a fix on than those of men. A typical female body has a 28-day cycle, divided into two parts of fourteen days each. The first part of the cycle occurs in the week on either side of ovulation. (Birth control pills lengthen this part of the cycle and compress the next.) A woman will tend to feel inspired here. She will grasp the big picture, see the importance of love, of family, of peace. She will sense the purpose of life and be on automatic here as far as nurturing human communication and connectedness. This inspirational segment is the easy, most enjoyable and upbeat portion of the female cycle.

The second part of a woman's cycle is emotional and expressive. It encompasses the week before and the week of menstruation. Here, instead of the big picture, a woman sees details, especially any that have been politely or conveniently swept beneath the carpet. She feels more introverted and can get picky and moody, irritating everybody including herself. This part of the cycle helps to keep a woman conscious of what is really going on in her life. If she has been untrue to herself about anything, she now can make that realization, for her true feelings will likely come bounding up.

Civilized society encourages a woman to squelch this part of herself. But when she does bury this emotionally expressive, seemingly inconvenient part of her cycle—and nature—she loses. As she drifts further from her true feelings and true self, she becomes parched, a rainless woman. She may also end up with a menstrual cycle which calls increasing attention to itself through physical or emotional discomfort.

The ideal way to treat the expressive part of the cycle is to respect the emotions which arise and let them have a voice, even while realizing they may be overblown in the moment. Later, examine what came up, sort it through to make sure the underlying message was received. The more out of touch a person is with this lively, juicy part of herself, the scarier it is to let it out, but the drier life eventually gets without it. While this part of a woman's cycle can be discomforting—nobody loves having to look at inconvenient issues—it can tell her the truth about her life and keep her on course.

MALE BODIES

Men have similar problems with not valuing the tricky-to-handle portions of their natural cycles. They pass through three discrete, approximately 18-day, segments in their overall 54-day cycle. The in-charge hormone here is no longer estrogen, but testosterone, which creates more physicality and aggression, as well as a less emotional, more mental field for men. Because current Western culture tends to value one, maybe two, parts of each man's normal cycle, individual men respond by consciously or unconsciously overriding those undesired parts of themselves. In addition to social pressures on them, many men like to pretend they are rational, considered beings not subject to cyclic mood changes—like women. These factors make recognizing and identifying male cyclical changes more difficult. But, just as with women repressing their emotionality, this male repression and denial creates dry, unbalanced men who are potentially dangerous. To be full, rich and whole, a man needs to experience each of the three major moods his cycles naturally bring to him. Then, he's got rhythm!

The first phase of a man's cycle finds testosterone high. This is an action-oriented, extroverted, and sexy 18-day period. We call it the aggressive part of the cycle. It is the easiest of the three segments to wake up to and identify. Women often notice that men smell particularly attractive during this period.[4] During this time men take on more projects and more risks. They may feel more romantic, protective and heroic; sometimes they become legends in their own eyes.

Knowing that aggression, like unrestrained sexuality, can often lead to trouble, modern Western man may attempt to repress this part of his cycle and this part of himself. Men don't want to be unconsciously starting wars or having their other head lead them for 18-days when this aggressive period rolls around. But that is not much of a probability, especially for the man who is likely to clamp down on this expression in the first place. The point is to be able to use this energy positively. When a man cuts off this part of himself, he is that much less vital, alive or fun; furthermore he is then prone to being sporadically and negatively run around by this aggressive side of himself. The men's movement is attempting to redress denial of this side by putting men back into enjoyment and harmony with the "hairy man" part of their natures.

This aggressive side to men is one that the feminists of the 70s and 80s tried to tame or knock out with varying degrees of fervor and success. No one wants to be with a pushy, insensitive or

---

4 When you sniff the back of his neck and it smells like ambrosia, you are here.

out-of-control guy, but again the real point is to handle these energies positively. Many women who have been frustrated with their stale mates appreciate the new liveliness engendered by men's groups—even when status quo is threatened.

The second segment in a man's cycle is characterized by intellectual behaviors, by thinking. A man now becomes analytical about his life, his relationships, his actions and times. He strives for understanding, making overviews as he goes. Suddenly he is communicating first and taking action later. Sex becomes more neutral here, not so important—but far from a dead issue.

This intellectual phase is the most acceptable part of the cycle to modern Western men, who often try to stretch its cool focus over the other two segments of their cycles. The desire to remain lofty, intellectual and in control at all times is understandable, but there are huge drawbacks to this onesidedness; men pay for it with emotionally barren lives.

The final 18-day period is an introverted, moody phase, an assimilative time. Turning inward, the man mulls over his life, his actions and times. What goes on here is a less conscious, more back-burner activity than the previous rational, intellectual phase. A man may become melancholy and cranky; ideally though, if he gets moody he will be reflecting on his internal states. This is a catch-up time, and a time to rest and prepare for the activity of the upcoming aggressive period. The energy of assimilation feels like winter energy, and can be about as dynamic as hibernation. In fact, a man will probably be sleeping more here and be somewhat withdrawn sexually.

This assimilative phase in the cycle is the one men resist most. It is also as much in emotion's lap as their body cycles place them. Like gray weather, this can be a pleasurable time; but unfortunately men in Western cultures are not conditioned to flow with it and brood. The training is to stay active and positive, quash those moods, get on top of them. Aside from Mr. Rogers, there are few cultural icons who help men understand the positive aspects of subjectivity, inertia and stewing around. Men who rethink this one enrich their lives, but it takes courage, just as it does for a woman to let her emotions speak when she is not sure what will come out or how major the consequences.

Notice that men's and women's cycles will overlap every month at new junctures, so that heterosexual couples can't synchronize into predictable moods or behavior patterns. How male and female approach each other and how they are received will vary, sometimes from week to week. Perhaps the most hazardous phasing is when the male is moody and assimilative and the female brooding and emotional; then neither has much objectivity, nor the bounce to rise above arguments or issues.

BUT MATRIARCHY!

Because of bodily strength and societal values, people long thought that women could never be men's equals. That view is now speedily changing, among women and men. The world is already rushing towards the sexual equality which will predominate on a generous portion of the globe during the 21st century. Pushing ahead even further in time, we see an upcoming matriarchal period, likely to last at least 1000 years, quite strongly in place by 2150. This is a period when those of you choosing women's bodies will have power and control over most social policies; women will have the primary say in government, politics, media and business, and over men.

How could it ever get from here to there? It is nearly impossible for people raised in male-dominated countries and worlds even to imagine the physically weaker female gaining control over the stronger, more aggressive male, but consider a sequence of events similar to this: Men are progressively seen as responsible for the problems the world is facing, especially when it becomes all too obvious that they are resistant to the clean-ups, changes in technology, politics and so on that are clearly necessary. They will be held guilty for high defense spending, huge deficits, leaking toxic waste dumps and the corruption of financial institutions and regulatory agencies. Women, who are untainted by these policies and scandals partially because they have not had power, will increasingly be the people insisting these messes be cleaned up and the people coming up with the proposals to do it. While they are at it, women will also improve the lot of the aged and the young. In fact, many of the leaders who will initiate and build the human-sized institutions mature souls want will be women.

The elevation of women over the next century will happen as part of a process where the modes in which women commonly operate will "suddenly" be seen as more valuable to society than the ways men operate. You can see hints of this already; for example, part and parcel of the current consciousness change is a shift away from hierarchical organizations with their one-up and one-down power situations. Many companies are already searching for ways to make work situations meaningful, mutually satisfying experiences. Businesses are starting to design structures based on shared power, mutual aid and trust, because that now looks stronger and more competitive. Running an organization by rank, or a country by social violence, will become less and less a viable option, for newer solutions will be glowing too attractively. Neither mature soul societies nor workers will be willing to put up with iron rule from the top.

Consensus building, now being explored because of Japanese success with it, is something women tend towards naturally, yet only recently was seen as a spineless, indecisive management style. Sharing information, instead of withholding it, talking frankly with people, complimenting them, these too are typical female ways of being which are beginning to have more coin in the management world. As values continue to change, women will more easily excel in the new atmosphere; they will feel safer about expressing their opinions. And, feeling free to be themselves will make them more powerful. Instead of straining to stick to the language of men and business, a woman's natural way of communicating will suddenly be seen to have advantages.

People in women's bodies suffer less from the illusion of control. As baby-bearers, women understand flowing with what life brings more intimately than men; they also tend to have more respect for life and less of the aggressive urge to dominate nature. As life-givers, women, in general, are more hesitant about war, even short simple ones with supposedly few downsides.[5] They keep communicating until they figure out other solutions to problems. For these reasons and more, the female sex is due to be viewed in an increasingly favorable light.

It is not too far from all this to a society that increasingly values women, their ideas and input, causing men to feel less innately intelligent and valuable. In this way, men gradually become the second sex. Lowered male self-esteem makes it easier to train them to stifle themselves, to be less active for their own good. And it takes their power. Make examples of the ones who don't fall into step; embarrass them, punish them, and fewer men will risk those same behaviors. Make men feel bad about themselves when they don't control their "primitive" impulses towards aggression and they become self-monitoring, and just like women before them, now unable to grasp their own capabilities. Because this switch will be happening in a mature soul world, it is unlikely society will get into the rougher, young soul control methods of the past—like the property confiscation and witch burning of feisty women.

It is from this sequence of changes like this that power will gradually fall back into female hands. We are not suggesting that women are morally superior or that in the 22nd century they are going to govern perfectly, peacefully, efficiently and with good feelings all around, but the world will run differently, more humanely in many aspects and certainly with more respect for nature. It will be crazy in new ways. People in men's bodies will be struggling with their "innate" limitations. Given the mature soul cli-

---

5 Women are not immune to the politics and rationales of war—Margaret Thatcher, Indira Gandhi and Golda Mier all led their countries into wars; they were all young souls.

mate, self-help books, groups and therapists will still be flourishing as they attempt to assist men to process their feelings of shame and inadequacy.

In the West, you have 20 years of major flux behind you, and ten years in front, where there still is chaos in how the sexes define themselves. In the quest for new balance, interesting karmas will be created as women and men experiment with new ways of being with each other.[6] This is one more reason that being alive in this time is as intense and exciting as it is. Your entire past history within common memory is being rewritten regarding men and women, with you the authors.

JAPAN: YOUNG WOMEN IN A MATURE WORLD

As mentioned previously, the current of consciousness is moving along at a faster clip than during prior soul age shifts. Music and other Western media carry messages far, fast and wide. A world population in communication with all its parts speeds personal and cultural change. The Japanese are very aware of what is going on in the U.S. and one result is that already some Japanese women find themselves unwilling to put up with traditional male dominance, especially in the form of traditional marriage.

Japan is an early young soul society. Women have until very recently been tightly under the male thumb, servants really, who dared not have opinions or ideas of their own. They raised children, cleaned, waited on, and basically said yes to everybody, especially males; not a high self-esteem situation. The Japanese have long considered that a woman was ruined, dead really, if not married by age 25. High tension still exists around this issue, but many women are doing the unheard of and choosing not to get married—this without the full array of career opportunities now available in the U.S. Yes, the men are in shock. They don't un-

---

6 Karma gets created when at least one participant feels intense about a certain situation, be it a quick robbery or 20 years of marriage. The real reason you "pay it back" is that each essence wants to "get" totally how that experience was for the other person by living it through in a body on the physical plane.

derstand what has hit them and are reacting in true young soul fashion by putting even more attention on their work and company.

These women, numbering as high as 20% in major cities, would rather focus on their own lives than lead the restricted life of a wife. To hazard never having a husband in a traditional society famous for sexism and social censure takes courage of the first degree. To buck group-think, humiliate your parents and risk being treated like a social leper is a big step even for an independent-minded young soul. It is an incredible change that women are making, especially given that society as a whole has barely pulled away from its baby soul herd-mind era.

Do you see what else is happening here? In this new mature soul world, even the women of the most powerful young soul country are able to angle for their own freedom and independent development. Japan, easily able to dominate world business, can no longer count on dominating its women. Nor, as it turns out, can it count on them to have enough babies to replace the current generation in the labor force. Interesting times.

The children Japan does produce are smothered with attention, clothes and toys. Children who are quickly given everything don't necessarily develop strong relational skills. Later, these youngsters are so pressured into performing at school that when their hormones start zooming they suppress normal adolescent craziness in order to pass tests. Adolescent emotional explorations are thus sacrificed on the altar of academic excellence. Remember that young souls like to excel, often whatever the cost, so it is not just demanding parents causing this to happen. But by this repression, teenagers further arrest relational development and often end up emotionally abridged. Developmental arrest is one reason why phenomenal numbers of middle-aged businessmen read sado-masochistic comics on the train during the morning commute; and why large numbers of women remain so childlike.

In Japan, you won't be seeing a maturation of the emotional

bonding between the sexes as you will in North America and other mature soul areas. The sexes will be getting more independent from each other, not closer. Mature souls wouldn't put up with this Japanese avoidance of stimulating relationships, but in a young soul country relationships and family systems are bound to dwindle in importance. On the other hand, all that energy being directed into education and business gives them an edge in the money world, which is where it's at for the young soul.

IN THE THIRD WORLD

We have previously discussed what happens to society when young soul men start getting born into heretofore baby and infant locales—watch out status quo! It is a rare young soul who will stay on the bottom for long, no matter how the deck is stacked against him.

Quite similarly, status quo takes it on the chin when young soul women start being born into these same societies because they aren't willing to be slaves either. To work hard, have little to show for it, no rights, and no hope of betterment becomes basically intolerable. No more resigned, mixed feelings about nine kids and a depressed guy who drinks the money away. Life starts reorganizing itself fast when young souls are around.

These women have little choice but to stand up for themselves. They will make men, laws and churches change. This will be a felt feminism, a drawing of lines. I am human and I am not putting up with that: So change. Men and society will slam doors on these women, but without much overall hope for success, particularly in Christian countries. In Islamic, Buddhist and Hindu countries, life for women is not quite so ripe for transformation.

Neither Latin America nor Africa will get particularly tumultuous because of the male-female restructuring that we expect. The underlying sense is that times have changed and people had better be moving along. Social programs, education, employers and husbands, fathers and boyfriends will all be shaping up as newly uppity women begin to change the climate for all women.

This reordering in the third world will be provoked by relatively small groups of lower-class (young soul) women. But given the times and the substantial strength, stamina and independent spirit of the young soul, the tide turns; not in a revolutionary manner and not even with the amount of chaos the U.S. experienced around this issue. But the tide turns. Women gradually and irrevocably gain power, safety and say-so in their lives. These women are less likely seeking career empowerment than a personal sense of power, security for their children and men, and improved communities.

Most South American countries will continue to have baby soul majorities, but the atmosphere for women will be slightly different. If the Catholic Church chooses not to support women in these changes, the church will lose adherents and power.

While Africa is set to remain primarily baby and infant, more young soul women will be born there too. Traditionally, Africa has seen greater independence in its female population than has Latin America, so this part of life won't be altering radically. Africa's influx of young soul women may want to forgo children, and instead create businesses and make money. They won't make huge changes in the way life looks for the average woman. Women's rights will be increasingly considered, though, and traditional childhood surgical practices like clitorectomy and excision of the labia will fall fairly rapidly out of style. In the wake of the devastation of Africa's populations, women will come into more local control.

As India moves forward in the decade, some of its young soul women are going to be courageously challenging the rules, hoping to gain political footage and increased autonomy and safety. We do not see a quick or dramatic change here, more a slow struggle often pushed to the back burner. India's social institutions are so intricately multi-layered and embedded that they are nearly impossible to (successfully) confront head on. Indian women have a fair chance of manifesting nearly equal rights and not-quite-equal opportunities by 2030. These male-female power issues take a long time to solve here, partially because the social training for women creates a great fear of independence.

The Indian women who intend to move the female sex forward will have to work hard and long, sifting through argument upon argument and the debris of lost battles. Most of the young soul women we see coming up are teenagers and younger now, but they are nearing 20%, sometimes 25% in the under-20 population, again depending on locale. They will have the independence of thought, the drive and the nerve of typical young souls, but will know they must move carefully, with persistence. The old ways won't disappear easily. This up-and-coming young soul country will stick with male rights and under-valuation of women for as long as it can. Right now, the push in India is towards creating a society where people, mostly men, can make it economically, and not towards a society that fully enfranchises women. India's citizens have had so little for so long that few can imagine a world with enough money, food or opportunities for all, men and women.

Nevertheless, as women slowly gain more power in India, the unconscious way life now operates will change. Women will start looking at life with an eye towards getting it handled, at rooting out the underlying causes of problems. Family size will be rethought, as well as the distribution of education, medical care, and wealth. And, women will be re-thinking traditional marriage in which a potential husband is paid handsomely to take a girl off her father's hands. Not only does this system humiliate and devalue women and leave them bought, vulnerable and exposed, at its worst it places their lives in danger. At least one thousand brides are killed each year, usually in poorly investigated "kitchen fires" where the woman is ignited; the husband can thus marry again and collect another bride price. Usually he won't have any trouble finding another father willing to pay and to potentially risk his daughter's life. The young soul crew would like to get this bit of tradition changed because it makes so many women's lives precarious.

In most of the Asian countries which remain popular baby soul gathering spots, tradition will remain tradition, women unquestioning. Neither will the position of women change rapidly in those countries striding into materialistic young soul phases. Singapore, Taiwan, South Korea, Thailand, none of these will be adjusting themselves much on women's issues. Economies in these countries will continue to perk, money will be easier to make and there will be an abundance of material goods to buy. Women will be more frequently educated and hold jobs, but basically these countries remain tradition-bound as far as how the sexes are viewed and treated. When either women or men manage to obtain any comfort financially, they will begin helping relatives to move up. Very few will be trying to fix society in order to provide the female sex with fairer breaks.

China, as usual, is running its own course. The government already insists that men and women are equal partners with equal rights and responsibilities. While women do receive nearly equal educations and are forbidden from becoming baby machines, Chinese society is still pervasively sexist. And it is not a big issue. Life between the sexes has strayed far enough from traditional paths for now. The main movement we see in China is towards democracy, meaning relief from bureaucracy and police as well as more freedom to do business and make money. Whatever elbow room women have gained over the last three decades appears to be enough to satisfy them for the next decade or so. Much needs to be done in China for it to become the world power it desires, hence casting a critical eye on a still-patriarchal system doesn't carry much interest.

RUSSIA, ETC.

The former Soviet Union was another populous society

where women supposedly had achieved equal status, rights and freedoms. Once again, actual reality is different, for with equality women ended up doing traditional tasks too and about twice the work of their men. They were factory workers or scientists too, and they were the people who stood in many lines for the day's supply of food, and then cooked it; they were the people who most evenings washed out the day's laundry in the bathtub and cleaned the flat. These women are worn and beginning to feel their resentment. To them, this extra burden was just one more insult from the monolithic system which ran their lives and was impossible to budge.

The current political unrest and chaos definitely makes it poor timing to address male-female issues. But, as life begins to find a new balance over the next decade, it will be seen that women have in fact gained more control over their lives and their men, without major squabbles. The main focus now is necessarily on political and economic issues, on how to cooperate and use freedom—but sexism gets worked out peripherally because of the flow of the times.

EUROPE

Both Northern Europe and the U.S. climbed out of rigid sexual stereotyping in the 70s and 80s. Because most European countries already had mature soul majorities then, the process was more gentle than in the U.S. Laws, customs and people changed while the sexes continued to enjoy their polarities. Women allowed themselves to keep their feminine allure and romanticism; many men retained their charm and gallantry. European men were not so beaten down, nor were the women so tough as in the U.S.

Southern Europe has yet to fix its traditional sexism, or to see much need. Greece and Italy, both with large mature soul populations, will continue to play with the divisions between the sexes, keeping the good-girl bad-girl dichotomy inflamed and their cat-calling, bottom-pinching males buoyant. The current set up is still too full of excitement, intensity and thwarted desires to let go. For now, essences being born into those countries want the craziness of life as it is. Even the astral plane is voting for status quo.

Spain has quite a different scenario. It is pushing into its young soul era with thousands of its girl children being born as warriors, nearly 40%. Mostly teenagers or younger now, they will eventually turn the men and the tight old system upside down, without much grace or tact.

With economies falling apart in Eastern Europe, furthering equality between the sexes is understandably near the bottom of most people's agendas. However, these countries are now being heavily exposed to Western media; this will provoke changes in attitude and behavior between the sexes. In the meantime, as Eastern Europeans desperately seek political and economic stability, increased rights for women will come along in their own good time. Those countries engaging in warfare will hold women's rights in abeyance for a longer period of time.

AUSTRALIA, ETC.

Australian women are definitely aiming for greater self-determination; while they may enjoy the macho of their men, they are after greater economic self-determination. The young soul woman here has swagger of her own. She wants to be able to put on her suit or overalls and prove she can run the bank or the ranch at least as well as the fellows. The hotter, more dramatic mature soul issues like rape, incest, family and societal violence will receive publicity here, but the urge of society to dig in and fix these behaviors is small for the present. Young souls don't want to have their sense of freedom impinged upon by "excessive" rules.

New Zealand, unlike the young soul Australia, is stretched between large numbers of baby and mature souls. Mature souls have most of the power and run the show in a comfortable, laid back sort of way. The baby souls add a stable, conservative element; nothing changes too fast. New Zealand is not an aggressive or competitive place, and few work too hard. Stable family situations are the norm and people feel safe, at home in their world. Women obtain enough respect and freedom already to make a restructuring of male-female behaviors unlikely. An essence now choosing New Zealand does so because a life in a comfortable, peaceful, non-hurried 20th-century place is what's desired.

VIOLENCE

Violence comes under scrutiny with this consciousness shift because the mature soul wants life to be right for everyone and for fairness to exist. That children are beaten, brutalized and raped is hard to face up to, but the mature soul does. These issues get talked about with an eye towards identifying and fixing the underlying social problems. Schoolchildren have begun to learn that it is not right for them to stay quiet if they are being hurt or sexually abused. It is only in the last fifteen years that a child anywhere would even have the vocabulary to make an accusation of child abuse.

Many people who were sexually maltreated as children are now being encouraged to let those memories to surface so that they can be processed and healed. Therapists are digging in, exploring all aspects (except for the karmic ones) of abuse, and getting keener about spotting symptoms of early abuse in clients whose memories of it are buried.[7] Childhood abuse is primal—it engenders lifelong pain and mistrust. Investigating all of this represents a huge shift in the power equations between men and women and between big people and little people.

Violence in the form of physical or sexual violence or even verbal abuse is something fewer are willing to blame themselves for. Women have been encouraging each other to pull out of destructive relationships, and not to assume their love for a man should (or ever could) heal him or cure a bad situation. Abused

---

[7] Even if your early childhood abuse had karmic elements to it, attempting to clear the sadness and rage out of your adult system is still beneficial.

women are learning to put themselves first, to gather up bruised self-respect and leave.[8] Women who have been pushed into sex are getting angry—instead of presuming somehow it was their own fault. College girls are sharing with each other, sometimes on bathroom wall "castration lists", the names of fellows who get rough and won't stop unwanted advances. Men are being forced to become more conscious about sex, since if they don't back off when a woman says no they they can be shamed, censured and prosecuted. Society is less and less willing to provide cover for these behaviors towards women—another result of the conscious-ness of the new mature soul world.

It is perhaps interesting to mention in passing that if a situa-tion exists in your family or neighborhood where violence may be occurring, you will be more inclined to overlook it, to put blinders on and not deal with it if it's a karmic payback going on. Fresh new karma being formed right in front of your nose smells about a hundred times worse than karma which is being wrapped up. People commonly feel much more passion about stopping new karma from being formed, and more wary about interfering with that which is being completed. Moral principles aside, your body and emotions will have you reacting to the differences very clearly.

Violence won't stop, but it will gradually recede. In fact, there may seem to be more violence short-term simply because it more frequently shows up for public discussion and condemna-tion. The day is not past where a woman reporting a rape may be poorly treated by police, doctors or the courts; but as women in-creasingly participate in those professions, shabby treatment will dwindle.

Violence in news reporting, novels, comic books, cartoons and television programming and films entered increasingly into human circuitry throughout the 70s and 80s. Starting with the

---

8 Well, the tricky part of this is that if you are in the middle of a karmic payback situation, usu-ally you don't find yourself leaving until the karma is complete and satisfied—even if you think you should have left years earlier. Nevertheless, it is smart to keep working on your self-esteem issues.

then-shocking violence of El Topo, films of the last two decades became progressively more violent. Rambo and dozens of other macho heroes of war, guts, guns, spears and bombs created odes to the dark side of (young soul) male individualism. Similarly to the way baby souls instinctively knew they had better jump up and fight abortion before time passed them by, young souls moved to get in their last licks before this testosterone-pumped stuff fell from favor. Thus, the orgy of film, television and literary violence arose out of the young soul's sixth sense that times were changing.

The 90s will see a turn from violent action in films and television. Once blockbuster big-name action films no longer guarantee megabuck returns, Hollywood will find higher moral ground and put its money and its mouth towards more creative, positive visions of life. Already it is producing a surge of after-death and reincarnation stories and is gearing up for more female "buddy" movies. Quite a change. As mature soul mentality takes charge, the consensus will be that it was horrible that so much violence was thrown at people, children particularly, and that more healthful ways to spend leisure time had better be found. Hollywood will change its focus, make more money and help the world realize a new future (at least while Los Angeles is well-functioning).

REGULATIONS FROM THE HEART

People are going to feel more heart-centered, family, community and relationship oriented. Mature souls sometimes have the urge to regulate everything to make sure every minute part of life falls into line with their ideals. Violence, for example, may be regulated out of films. In the quest for a fair, people-oriented society, mature souls will many times regulate and legislate to make their vision a reality. In Germany, for instance, stores legally aren't allowed to be open evenings so that store employees can be home with their families. This makes it hard for singles, or couples who both work, to buy groceries or anything else. Saturday shopping is murderously crowded—but people are home with their families on week nights which makes this mature (and baby) soul society happy. In Berkeley, neighborhood streets are stopped, started and blockaded to create a confusing, time-consuming pattern motorists avoid, thus keeping the neighborhoods basically traffic-free and more pleasant. Main traffic arteries are jammed most of the time.

Mature soul societies will delicately and indelicately regulate many heretofore "unconscious" behaviors. Already you have stronger rape, sexual harassment and domestic violence laws, stronger protection for children, stronger anti-discrimination laws in the workplace and in the banking system. The enforcement of these laws is starting to encourage changes in thinking and behavior.

Pornography has been under sharp scrutiny for years. There is little doubt films which are demeaning to women will come under assault in the coming years. Promises of self-regulation probably won't do. Regulating ways of being and living is difficult without cutting into the freedom of action many people now enjoy. The mature soul, while trying to work these matters through carefully, often feels that a "small" loss of freedom for the sake of society's greater good is worth the cost. Some policies and laws are bound to look picky, silly or overblown, and will need continuing revision until people are generally satisfied.

WOMEN'S RIGHTS AND THE NEW WORLD ORDER

Laws that support women and aim to equalize rights will be promoted, worldwide, by the western countries because the political benefits start to be clear. When women get support, population growth goes down. Support of women also cuts into machismo, which then cuts into power trips, dictatorships and wars. When women start getting a fairer shake, their self-esteem grows, they get more authority in their voice, and they tend to influence their men towards higher degrees of cooperation in the world.

CHAPTER 9

The Mending World Servers

Everything that lives,
Lives not alone, nor for itself.
—William Blake

Get yourself into balance and move in a sacred manner now.
Learn how to will things into existence, learn how to make
things happen. That's part of being a spiritual warrior.
Don't "just exist".
—Sun Bear

WORLD SERVICE

The reason we channel information through to you is love; sharing this information about universal patterns and dynamics is a form of service, which in turn helps us with our own growth. Prepared with foreknowledge, you can remain more centered during many of these upcoming Earth events. That then gives you a better crack at healing the planet. As individuals you are powerful in where you choose to put your energy, in what you promote.

One intention of our work is to expand your boundaries of consciousness so that you can become more active and empowered in the world, and less reactive to it. Human consciousness is changing to be sure, and nearly of its own accord. But to mend the earth and keep the best scenarios open, action is required to reshape politics, economics, business and technology, and the thinking of the average guy and government. Life is going to get reshuffled: it is your individual energy and effectiveness over the next ten years that will make a huge difference to the outcome. Many of you have the internal sense that you are part of the new surge of world servers: your inner voices bid you to heal the planet. We hope our sharing of this information will give you the solid confidence to forge ahead into the areas of life you would like to see re-birthed.

While the business-as-usual machine is still steaming along, momentum is on its side which makes changing course difficult. But as time moves on, the old system will grow shaky and vulnerable; then it is all up for grabs. Consequently, the world will be more open to your point of view, ideas and projects in a much more generous way than now. Your intent and your actions can suddenly make interesting, influential differences.

As you form groups, you strengthen your hand. Associations of people with common purposes and ideals enhance each individual's energy and have a powerful (and faster) impact on the world. If you choose to work in groups, be sure to keep your integrity intact. Remain true to yourself and to your deeply held values, speaking up for them when necessary. The mature soul can be subject to intense idealism; an old soul's value will occasionally lie in being able to calm things down and create more tolerance for differing points of view.

To participate at high levels in the outside world, you must stay in touch with your inner world, heal your old wounds and heal your fresh wounds. Ask your higher self to feed you light; ask your spirit guides for love and healing and strength. Sense the divine in the Earth. Make up rituals to greet change in your life and change in the seasons. These are the simple ways to keep yourself fresh and inspired through these times. If you get too lost in the rush of events to be quiet and be with your inner self, you lose power, effectiveness and beauty.

INSPIRED YEARS

One totally pleasant piece of news we can give you is that a sense of inspiration and emotional connectedness will be worlds easier to find, beginning in 1993. The months and years will start to have a high, very fine emotional quality to them. This feeling will be in the air for several years whatever the outside circumstances, terrific or harsh. More than usually, people will be experiencing higher-minded feelings, idealism, love and heartfelt compassion for others. Family values get a big uplift and relationships will be kinder and mellower. Even on the street, there will be more polite and loving kindness. You will find yourself enjoying tender connections with people—with much less rushing about!

In years so much influenced by higher feelings and thoughts, people tend to feel uplifted and experience more expansive and beautiful states of consciousness than usual. Old and mature souls will value and enjoy this energy the most. The older soul easily basks in the warmth these expanded states allow. Younger souls like to play with the energy of separation and do not particularly want to see all life as a cozy, interrelated unit.

This is a very special coming together of the human family. People will be looking at justice; removing obstacles to people's self-sufficiency will be seen as important. What is the fair way to divide resources in a city, country or world? It is one thing to think about fairly dividing intangibles like education and health services and another level entirely to think about dividing up material, like chickens or gasoline. Happily these higher center experiences allow people and societies to jump realities, to see connections and possibilities and thus break down mechanical habit patterns from the past. Not just old-time liberal politics here, but higher truths coming to the forefront of people's minds to get some practical handling. Truth and pragmatism are in the air together, an auspicious combination.

Most years have a strong, underlying influence from either the intellectual center, the emotional center or the moving center. For example, 92 is an intellectually influenced year in which many individuals will find themselves sorting through their lives with newly clear thinking. Politicians are suddenly required to come up with facts, programs and more honesty than usual since emotional slogans and negative ads won't carry the day. Occasionally there are also catch-up years, which are influenced by the instinctive center, as well as these relatively rare higher-centered years.[1]

RESPONSIBILITY

There are no shoulds and oughts. Being responsible means responding ably and competently, tuned into your sense of what is right for you in any given situation. Being responsible entails being in integrity with yourself: sometimes that means surrender, but it can also mean persevering; sometimes it means taking outward action, other times going inward. No right, no wrong, just going with that inner sense of what is true for you.

One common and fairly effective response people will have to the onslaught of events will be an increased sense of prudence. You can see some of that energy already in the "new frugality" gaining popularity and media attention in the U.S. People are not only spending less, they are consciously putting attention on appreciating life's simpler pleasures. Conspicuous consumption already carries less status and will quickly—even more quickly than smoking did—succumb to social pressure. Eventually this means less Wal-Mart, not just less Neiman Marcus.

Prudence inclines you to use forethought, to be careful. It makes you value temperance and centeredness—very different

---

[1] 93, 94 and 95 are the three higher-centered years.

qualities than the 80s called forth! This careful, thoughtful stance will help you stay relaxed through the 90s, for in knowing that you are grounded, you can trust yourself to stay centered. This aids survival, and it helps your inner responses and actions be from the deepest aspects of your nature.

Combine prudence with higher-centered times and you have an interesting result: people fairly quickly find the heartfelt values they need to sustain themselves. Young souls will still want to equate net worth with self-worth, but not so many people will be willing to play that game with them. Mature and older souls are able to quickly let go of consumerist values—and actually, if you flow with the times, there is little choice. There just isn't as much material stuff to play with! Where do you get enduring satisfaction, what brings it? Redoing the living room didn't bring it, neither did the sexy red car with its four-year price tag. Now it gets down to people, love and service; to doing work you love and doing your work with love; to spending time with the people you care about; and to pitching in with projects that you care about. You make the beauty in your life. People are ripe to discover what life can be about when it isn't mostly about more stuff.

VALUES CLARIFICATION FOR GOVERNMENT

The questions first-world populations need to be asking start being asked. How many material things do you need to be happy? Is it OK to want the things that also "happen" to poison the world? Is it OK to eat when the third world cannot? Clarifying planetary values becomes the task at hand.

This new prudence creates new values for government too; governments won't be allowed to bungle their money either. Measuring a nation's health and vitality by increases in gross national product will seem archaic. As it gets perfectly clear that more products and more production aren't necessarily any better for a nation than they are for individuals, new yardsticks will be found for gauging a country's progress. .

Changed circumstances will force governments to prioritize expenditures and spend only on what sifts out as necessary and worthwhile in light of changed circumstances. One item bound to be near the top of funding priorities will be finding solutions to environmental toxicity. Financing for glamorous scientific projects such as billion-dollar super accelerators or space labs and shuttles will probably have to wait. Cleaning up technologies so the planet can heal can't wait. This means lowering carbon dioxide emissions and putting money into solar and wind technologies, getting them up and going. It foreshadows new kinds of cars. It implies finding ways to keep forests healthy and threatened species alive. And it may mean immune-system enhancement programs for all living things.

New values are likely to reward people who blow the whistle on out-of-integrity industries. While whistle-blowers currently have promises of protection and job security, reality falls far short and they often suffer tremendously for their truth-telling acts of courage. Times are changing though—even ecologists will be better treated before long. Governments will likely start raising money and making moral points by meaningfully penalizing illegal or careless activities on the part of industry. No more puny fines and slaps on the wrist—times are too idealistic for politicians to get away with this without jumping into very hot water themselves.

STEWARDSHIP

There are many ways to care for the Earth. Making lifestyle changes is one; voicing your concerns about activities which will poison your air and water or shrink your forests is another. Fighting to protect rural areas and wild areas is another action you can take. Educating people, children especially, to treasure the Earth is yet another way you can honor your planet. These are but a few of the many outer actions you could possibly take. Always do what interests you, what grabs you, for that is your part to do.

On a more personal level, perhaps you decide to plant trees over your lot or neighborhood or town; perhaps you take a piece of land and nurse it back to health, making it as abundant and special as you can. Maybe you study non-chemical, life-promoting ways to garden and then grow vegetables and flowers—and discover devas in the process. Or perhaps you find yourself embellishing a particular area with stacks of rocks, buried crystals and a handmade bench, making the land feel more special and sacred to you. What is your way of connecting deeply with the Earth? You will want to find it, for therein lies the healing.

About the Author

For the last sixteen years, Joya has worked in the healing arts as a vision therapist, a life/death transitions counselor and a nutritional and psychic consultant. She has been channeling since the mid-seventies. When she was introduced to Michael in 1984, the process deepened immensely. The last seven years have been dedicated solely to working with Michael and getting the Michael material out to as many people as possible.

Author of the now-classic, refreshing take on human psychology and behavior, *The World According to Michael: An Old Soul's Guide to the Universe,* and a co-author of *The Michael Game,* Joya also wrote the current event column, "Michael Views the News," which appeared for several years in the quarterly magazine, *The Michael Connection.* Beginning in 1993, her channeling work will also appear in *Spirit Speaks* magazine.

Joya currently divides her time between writing, clients, national and international travel for workshops and channeling, and novels, gardening, friends, one special man, and the occasional letter to the editor or plea to city government.

For information about personal channeled readings (which can be done by telephone or through the mail) and personality trait (overleaf) charts showing where you, or your friends, fit into the Michael system, you may write to her c/o Emerald Wave Publishing Company, Box 969, Fayetteville, AR 72702.

More MICHAEL Books

The World According to Michael
by Joya Pope $10.95
This is the starter book of choice and the one to share
with friends. Explains roles, soul ages, personality
overleaves, task companions and essence twins.

Upcoming Changes: The Next Twenty Years
by Joya Pope $12.95

Tao to Earth
by Jose Stevens $11.95
Michael's special teachings about relationships and
communication. Life tasks, intimate companions,
support groups, karma.

Earth to Tao
by Jose Stevens $11.95
The sequel. Spiritual awakening, guides, animal
helpers and healing techniques.

Michael's Gemstone Dictionary
by J. H. David, channeled by JP Van Hulle $18.95
Energies and usage of 500 minerals. Find out why
you're attracted to your favorite stones, and which ones
keep you positive. An amazingly valuable reference book.

The Michael Game $ 7.95
This collection of articles contains "Whales and Dolphins
as Sentient Beings" by Joya Pope plus "Confessions of
a Walk-in", "101 Questions to Ask a Channel" and more.

Michael: The Basic Teachings
by JP Van Hulle, A. Christaaen and M.C. Clark $11.95
A clear, well-organized metaphysical primer, full of
delightful, informative illustrations.

The Michael Handbook
by Jose Stevens and Simon Warwick-Smith $11.95
A 350 page reference book revealing the foundation
of the Michael teachings in depth.

Ask for any of these Michael books at your bookstore
or order direct from:
Emerald Wave
Box 969 Fayetteville AR 72702

•20% discount on 5 books or more•

Send to:

Name_____

Street_____

State & Zip_____

Title:	#copies	Price	Total
The World According to Michael	_____	$10.95	_____
Upcoming Changes	_____	$12.95	_____
Tao to Earth	_____	$11.95	_____
Earth to Tao	_____	$11.95	_____
Michael's Gemstone Dictionary	_____	$18.95	_____
The Michael Game	_____	$7.95	_____
Michael: The Basic Teachings	_____	$11.95	_____
The Michael Handbook	_____	$11.95	_____
		Subtotal	_____
5 books or more *only*, less 20% discount			_____
		Subtotal	_____
Postage, 1st title $1.50, additional titles $1.00 *each*			_____
AR residents add appropriate sales tax			_____
Total, check or money order			_____

Thank you for your order
Bookstores—order direct from: Bookpeople, New Leaf,
Moving Books, Baker and Taylor or The Rainbow Collective.